CONTENTS

PREFACE

◉

E very author can only hope that the content of his or her work will generate enough interest to connect with people. I have been fortunate enough to work directly with the public for more than a decade and witness the deep personal connection that brain health can make. My work across the United States has taught me several lessons, including the need to make sure my message is personal and is felt on a personal level by the audience. Second, people are genuinely interested in learning about their brains, and for most, our interaction is an introduction into the miracle of their brain. Third, people are willing to change behavior to promote their health, but that change does not occur unless informed by the why and the how behind the change. Fourth, millions of baby boomers are now caregivers for parents who have dementia, and these caregivers do not want to suffer the same misfortune; they want to preserve access to their life stories. Finally, due to current public interest in health and health care, there is recognition that a proactive lifestyle toward health is important, particularly for the brain. Together, these lessons have motivated me to write this book—to connect more with people about the most personal of all stories, their brain health and the brain health of their loved ones.

As a clinical neuropsychologist, I have cared for hundreds, and probably thousands, of patients who suffer from diseases and conditions of the brain ranging from depression, mania, schizophrenia, and substance abuse to dementia associated with Alzheimer's disease, stroke, Parkinson's disease, tumors, epilepsy, and head injury. These and other afflictions of the brain provide a real picture of the significant loss that can occur when the brain is damaged. There is a realization that the brilliance of the brain is, at the same time, fragile. It is from the loss of brain capability that a deeper appreciation of the brilliance and gift that is the brain emerges. It can also be the motivation to learn more about your brain and to begin the lifelong work toward brain health.

I have had the wonderful opportunity to speak to thousands of people from diverse sectors of society all across the United States and beyond about the human brain. My work and my message is to provide information on the basics of the human brain, how the brain operates and can be shaped by environment, and how my brain health lifestyle can be a guide to follow to promote brain health. As you read along, you will find that this book is written in a personal, informative, and fun manner so that everyone can benefit by learning more about their brain health.

From feedback I have received on presentations delivered to small groups in basements of buildings and audiences of more than five thousand people, I have learned that the public is very interested and enthusiastic about brain health. The message has found its way to the United Nations, the National Press Club, major media outlets, newspapers and magazines, the Internet, and new business start-ups and into the hallways of education, health care, corporate America, libraries, health insurance, and retail. I've spent many hours speaking to reporters and audiences about the miracle of the human brain, and I've written several books on the topic. A lot of what drives this mission is my firm belief that it is critical to take what we learn in the lab and from research and communicate it and apply it to the general public, which is why I approach brain health from the perspective of lifestyle.

As the brain is the center of our identity, it is easy to understand why people are so interested. Most people enjoy learning about themselves and will work to improve their health if they are told how. This book is a major step toward taking my message of brain health to a larger audience and instilling in them the idea that there is a miracle sitting within our heads that enables our every thought, emotion, and behavior.

We know more now about the human brain than at any other time in our history. We will continue to learn, and we certainly have much to learn. However, it is now abundantly clear that many stimuli in our everyday environment can shape both the structure and function of our brain. We now believe the human brain is directly affected by the types of environments we are exposed to on a daily basis. For some individuals, an enriched environment can literally promote the health of the brain, while others may cope with more traumatic stimuli, such as war. Regardless, it is critical that we all understand that our brains will be shaped by the type of environmental input, or stimuli, that we encounter on a daily basis.

Journey to Becoming a Brain Health Ambassador

I was less than twenty years of age when I began working as an activity assistant in a local nursing home. The home was new and had a specialized wing for persons suffering from Alzheimer's disease. This was quite progressive in 1983. It was also my first "real job" for which I got a paycheck. My role was to work specifically on the Alzheimer's unit and to construct a research project that focused on an activity program with the persons living on the unit. We were able to show that Alzheimer's patients who remain involved in social programming can evince a decline in depression over a period of time. The study was presented at a national conference and published. My memory of the time I spent on the Alzheimer's unit, however, was much more personal and meaningful with regard to my early impressions of how the brain functions.

There was a gentleman living on the unit who became agitated at times, and he would try to "elope" off the unit. In fact, on occasion he would be found in the parking lot walking away from the building. Obviously, this was a major safety concern, and staff needed to be vigilant to this man and his behavior. I was asked to try and modify the "elopement," a clinical term we use in the field to describe someone who tries to get away from their unit. The person may or may not have a logical reason to leave the unit or building. Regardless, it is a serious concern due to the obvious safety risks for someone who is confused traveling in an unsupervised manner.

My first thought and feeling about this challenge was fear. I probably was afraid that the man would not cooperate with me and that I would fail. During one episode when he was walking away from the building, I approached him and asked him where he was going. He replied that he was going to his farm to tend to his crops. It turns out he was a farmer by trade, and his memory loss placed him back at this stage of his life. He had an accurate memory, but the context for that memory was no longer valid, and in fact, he had not worked in more than thirty years. I listened to him, and although he was agitated, I suggested to him that his farm was the other way, pointing toward the back of the building where his room was, and that I was happy to walk with him to the farm. He seemed to be pleased with my suggestion, and we walked safely back to the unit where he lived. I made sure we started a garden on the patio, and this gentleman was now in charge of growing tomatoes and other vegetables for residents living in the home. Of course, this experience was significant to me and taught me a great deal about Alzheimer's, memories, passions, and how to modify agitation by redirecting the agitated energy into purposeful pursuits.

On the same unit lived a friendly older female who suffered from Alzheimer's and was often sitting with others engaged in some activity. I noticed she would occasionally sit on her own, and at times she was tearful. I noticed this behavior tended to occur around dinnertime, a period of the day when some persons with Alzheimer's can demonstrate increased agitation. This behavior is often referred to as "sundowning." We do not know why this occurs, and we struggle to change the behavior when it does occur.

I sat next to the woman and asked her why she was crying. She explained to me that she was upset that she could not get home to cook for her children, that they were going hungry. Once again, a memory that was accurate was simply out of context. This woman did cook for her children for many years. The problem was that she had not cooked for her children for many years, as they were all grown and independent. Alzheimer's placed this woman into a time frame that was no longer real. Her emotions were real, and she felt very sad. I asked her to go with me to the kitchen area, where she helped me make some drinks to serve to the other persons living on the unit. This seemed to make her feel better and to grant her the role of traditional mom that she missed so dearly.

Several years later, I accepted a position as director of an aging and research center, where we conducted applied research and programming for nearly a thousand older adults living in a continuum of care. There was a large population of persons who suffered from Alzheimer's. I recall a husband walking into my office one day and breaking down in tears as he described his desperate efforts to connect with his wife, whom he loved. His emotional plea to me to bring her back continues to resonate with me today. I felt helpless as I tried to comfort this good man.

These are typical stories that are too real and very moving. This is what Alzheimer's is; in the real world, it is not the academic and clinical definition of plaques and tangles. Alzheimer's and other brain diseases steal our soul, our spirit, and our identity. Neurodegenerative diseases attack our life story, the most precious gift we have. Anyone who works on the front line with persons suffering from Alzheimer's knows these experiences and stories well. These experiences showcase the devastation that Alzheimer's can cause to a healthy brain and the emotional discord that relates to memories that are out of context and no longer attached to real time. Families are emotionally drained as they struggle with observing or caring for their loved one who is no longer connected to real time because memory is impaired, and memory requires some sense of the past and the present. Having these experiences with Alzheimer's patients also permitted me the opportunity to connect with them even though their brains were compromised and confused. The brain is brilliant enough to provide pathways of connection that enable emotional stability and calming. The brain will offer clues about the emotion and about the desire of the person. The human brain never stops its ability to be brilliant, even in the midst of a progressive degenerative disease such as Alzheimer's.

A more personal experience that hits closer to home is my relationship with my brother Robby. Robby is now fifty-three and was diagnosed with a pervasive developmental disorder when he was an infant. The doctors never were able to determine the cause for his disability, and some advised my parents to place him in an institution, advice my parents fortunately rejected. Robby suffers mental retardation, seizure disorder, and other neuropsychiatric illnesses. He lived at home for the first thirty-five years of his life, attended a school, but otherwise was dependent for basic activities of daily life. He then moved to a community living arrangement, where he continues to live and thrive today. As Robby is seven years older than me, I learned a tremendous amount about behavior and brain function growing up with him well before my academic training in neuropsychology. I recall trying to understand why Robby would get upset, and I also recall feeling bad when others made of him. These experiences guaranteed I would never make fun of anyone who was different or had difficulty.

Anyone who works with people with mental retardation understands quickly how important the frontal lobe is to brain function. As the chief executive officer of the entire brain, the frontal lobe organizes, choreographs, and initiates behavior in beautiful harmony. It also filters emotions, such as passion, rage, anger, and driven states, so behavior is expressed appropriately. When functioning in a normal way, the frontal lobe permits a healthy balance of mood and behavior. When disturbed, the frontal lobe expresses a variety of emotions that can range from mania to depression to an inability to control rage or temper. Some persons with mental retardation can display the disturbed version of frontal lobe function, and it is generally up to the caregiver to try and modify the behavior through routine and calm reassurance. All of us like routine.

My early observations of Robby and the many residents with Alzheimer's disease taught me a tremendous amount about human behavior, brain disease, and the importance of bringing calm to a chaotic brain. Each brain is capable of being comforted even though it may exist in a state of confusion and agitation. One interesting thing about the human brain is that it maintains ability and skill even when disease and disability are present. The man with Alzheimer's was able to grow tomatoes and vegetables, the woman with Alzheimer's was able to cook and serve under supervision, and Robby is employed and takes wonderful trips to other cities even though he has a documented mental age of three. Ultimately, Robby has provided his entire family with a gift of humility and love, and a reminder that with love from family, anything is possible. All of these individuals provide loved ones the ongoing lesson of what is really important in life, and they help us to prioritize our "stuff" in meaningful ways. Neural plasticity, the brain's ability to be shaped by environment, is a miracle that gets nourished with proper environmental input regardless of health or disease. Understanding what that input is and applying it across the life span is the challenge and purpose of a proactive brain health lifestyle.

THE BRAIN HEALTH LIFESTYLE

Engage in something new and complex for you today, make a new friend, eat a delicious meal that includes salmon, stop to enjoy the moment or engage in prayer, and walk around your block. Simple tips like these offer a few of the easy changes we can make in our daily routine to begin the process of living a proactive brain health lifestyle. The chapters that follow provide more examples of brain-healthy behaviors for you to consider and to add to your new brain health lifestyle.

The primary message of this book is that we should seek the types of environments that promote brain health. It is from these environments, rich in the novel and complex, that our brains will thrive and build brain reserve to combat the potential presence of neurodegenerative diseases, such as dementia. This underscores the importance of my proactive brain health lifestyle to help the brain delay the onset of neurodegenerative diseases like Alzheimer's.

I have been witness to so many who have lost access to their life stories and therefore have become disconnected from their loved ones. It is from these experiences that my work on the planet is now focused on helping everyone maintain as healthy a brain as possible. This is the rallying call and the personal message. This book is about you. I hope the message of this book motivates you to love your brain and to begin the process of caring for it from this day on.

INTRODUCTION

You have no greater asset than your life story. It must be shared with
your next great generation, the little ones in your life.

◉

Sitting across the table from a person struggling to recall his
name can be an unsettling experience. Perhaps even more
difficult is the realization on the faces of the family members
that their father or grandfather is no longer capable of recog-
nizing them and in some ways has forever been disconnected
from them. Brain disease such as Alzheimer's causes daunting
experiences. It is at these moments that we can understand the
sheer brilliance and, at the same time, the fragility of the human
brain. It is your brain, after all, that contains and expresses your
identity, enables your connection to others, creates and stores
your memories, and most important, tells your life story. This
book is written from the deep emotional reality that exists from
sitting at that table hundreds of times in my life. It represents
my attempt to provide a tangible guide for preserving access
to our identity, to our loved ones, to our life story. And while
the brain is fragile, it is also the most magnificent system ever
designed, capable of more than we can presently know and
deserving of a lifetime's dedication to health.

Watching a person who has been affected by a brain illness or condition is both difficult and enlightening. It is not uncommon to see a person suffering from a devastating brain illness cope with amazing fortitude and courage. At the same time, the signs and symptoms of brain disease can indeed be life-changing for the patient and those family members and friends who surround the patient. In my work, I have helped patients who have lost the ability to speak, to walk, to behave appropriately, to see or hear, and to remember. These are not simply functions lost because of a particular disease or insult to the brain—they represent a loss of part of the person. In the case of memory loss, the literal identity of the person may be lost. It does not get more personal that that! It is also important for me to state that my patients have helped me to understand that all of us can appreciate life and that it is so important to stop our hurried lives and enjoy the moment, to express ourselves to those we love, and to realize that today may be our last.

The human brain is the most brilliant and magnificent system ever designed. Every now and then the brain will express its sheer brilliance, though we tend to view some manifestations of this brilliance as "abnormal" or as a psychiatric disorder. I often use the example of *Rain Man*, the wonderful movie that stars Dustin Hoffman as a man who suffers from autism with a savant ability to mentally calculate the probability of a certain card being drawn from six decks of cards.

When it comes to the mind, there is nothing that now exists and there will never be anything built that comes close to the complexity of the human brain, and that is based on the little we know about the brain today. We underestimate the power of the human brain on a consistent basis. Despite our tendency to sit in awe of the latest technology or gadget, the most impressive portable and wireless system is the human brain, which is capable of things we cannot even imagine yet.

It is from this context and appreciation of the human brain that a deeper discussion can occur about why and how we care for this part of our being. Your brain contains your identity, your very being, your potential for personal development, and perhaps the innovation or idea that will forever change the lives of millions. Your brain builds over the course of your lifetime your personal life story, the most precious gift you have and one that needs to be shared with others whom you love. There is perhaps no greater untapped resource in the universe than the human brain. Cultures from the beginning of humankind have neglected the brain's importance and unique distinction. It is time to shift our viewpoint to awaken a wonderful interest in the human brain and a lifestyle that promotes brain health.

THE POWER OF YOUR BRAIN

Sitting inside our heads is the greatest system in the universe— a real miracle. We need to move beyond a perception of the human brain as an academic or clinical entity to one that is deeply personal. Indeed, we need to embrace this part of our being, the core of who we are, and learn about it. From an understanding of the basics of our brain, we can begin the process of caring for it and promoting its health. Brain health is a two-step process: (1) education on the basics of your brain and (2) making the process a deeply personal one that enables you to understand why you are spending time and energy following a brain health lifestyle.

Brain health recognizes the brain as a dynamic and malleable system that is shaped by environment across the entire life span. It is a way of life that is dedicated to exposing the brain to enriched environments, to the complex and novel, and to building brain reserve over a lifetime. Brain health recognizes the importance of a proactive process, and it does not recognize artificial age thresholds, as your brain does not know or care how old you are, and it does not adhere to the notion of "critical periods of brain development" unless life itself is that period. Brain health champions a proactive and lifelong approach, a lifestyle that will not only help to develop a healthy brain but will maximize your opportunity to delay the onset of neurodegenerative disease. Brain health is ultimately your commitment to maintaining access to your story with a deep desire to share that story with the next great generation.

I have spent the past decade studying the literature on brain health, keeping abreast of new developments in the area, and integrating this fragmented information into a practical application. The result, for me, has been a solid foundation for promotion of brain health that includes an understanding of the neurophysiological aspects of neural plasticity and the cognitive construct of "brain reserve."

There have been a relatively high number of research studies that correlate certain behaviors with reduced risk of dementia, what I refer to as "brain health." My work has been dedicated to organizing and integrating all of this information so that the field of neuropsychology and brain health can go from theory to real-world application. As you will see in the pages ahead, my intent is to provide you with a tangible and proactive lifestyle that promotes brain health through building brain reserve.

How to Get the Most Out of This Book

I have championed a brain health lifestyle that is proactive, research based, and built from the lessons learned from animal brain research many years ago as well as current cutting-edge research on the human brain. My brain health lifestyle consists of five critical components that I refer to as "the five slices of the brain health pie." These include socialization, mental stimulation, physical activity, spirituality, and nutrition. Each is equally important, as they reflect the fact that we are integrated and complex organisms and that we do not function optimally in a fragmented manner. Within each of these five areas, I have outlined research-based activities that have been proven to promote brain health. By including some of these activities across the five slices of brain health on a daily basis, you can begin the process of promoting the health of your brain and potentially delay the onset of neurodegenerative disease!

The purpose of this book is to educate you on the basics of your brain, to create an urgency to treat your brain as the most important part of your being, and to show you how to implement a proactive brain health lifestyle. I will give you the tools you need to encourage brain health and combat progressive neurodegenerative diseases such as Alzheimer's and related dementias.

Think of this book as an important guide that provides you with a unique approach to brain health that is comprehensive, integrated, and lifestyle oriented. It combines state-of-the-art neuroscience with principles of human behavior and offers practical tips to promote brain health. This book is built on the premise that lifestyle is critical to brain health—that the human animal will not change behavior unless he or she personalizes the message and understands the why behind the what.

The book champions the promotion of brain health across all sectors of society and illustrates its application to the education system, health care system, corporate and business world, religion, home, and ultimately the individual. Indeed, the message of this book is deeply personal and a call to action from the individual to society at large. Brain health unites all of us as humans toward a grand outcome—the ability in our twilight years to share our life stories with the little ones in our lives.

After reading *Save Your Brain*, you will know more about the human brain than most. More important, you will know what behaviors are critical to promoting your own brain health and how environmental input can literally shape the structure and function of your brain. This knowledge will help you take the steps to change your current lifestyle and adopt the proactive lifestyle for brain health. This is not easy, and it is not a "quick fix" but a lifelong process that will be challenging. If you commit to your brain health, it's a lifestyle change that is doable. I have found personal satisfaction in my own behavioral change as I work to integrate brain health into my life. I must admit that I have setbacks and frustrations, but that is the price of positive and healthy behavioral change.

These days, larger corporations are becoming more and more aware of brain health and how it affects their employees. I have worked with a company that has been very creative in applying different aspects of the brain health lifestyle with the workforce; it has been fun and informative—brain health promotion should be fun. It is time for you to embrace your brain and take proactive steps outlined in this book to maximize its health, but first let us assess your brain health by taking the following inventory.

YOUR PERSONAL BRAIN HEALTH INVENTORY

As you will learn in the following chapters, your brain is a highly dynamic system that will react to the types of input you feed it. From this perspective, you can appreciate how much control you have regarding the potential health of your brain. You may finally begin to focus on the greatest system ever designed in the history of the universe—your brain! The first step for your brain health lifestyle is to understand its five critical parts:

- Socialization
- Physical Activity
- Mental Stimulation
- Spirituality
- Nutrition

It is helpful to review these parts of your current lifestyle to better understand the positive and negative aspects for your brain health. Take the following assessment and find out your baseline score. It is important to be honest and to understand this is simply a guide to give you an idea of where you are right now. Results are not scientific and are meant to help guide your brain health lifestyle. Do not be alarmed if you give your current lifestyle a low grade. You have not been educated by society about the importance of your brain, and you have not been informed about brain health. That is about to change!

The following survey uses research-based information to help you measure your progress regarding implementation of your own brain health lifestyle. The survey is to be completed prior to starting your brain health program to obtain a baseline score and to be repeated every three months to document your progress. I have included step-by-step directions to calculate different scores for your assessment and what the scores mean to you. Each score is based on a total percentage of 100, with higher scores meaning a better brain health lifestyle and lower scores suggesting work or change is needed in particular parts of your brain health lifestyle. This is not scientific and is meant to provide you with an empirical measure of your brain health lifestyle.

Social Domain

Circle the response that best describes your behavior during the past three months.

	SCORE
1. I eat one meal with my family/friends every day.	5 points
I eat one meal with my family/friends weekly.	3 points
I do not eat meals with anyone.	0 points
2. I have joined two or more new groups this year.	5 points
I have joined one new group this year.	3 points
I have not joined any new group the past year.	0 points
3. I have started more than one hobby in the past year.	5 points
I have started one new hobby in the past year.	3 points
I have not started a new hobby in the past year.	0 points
4. I speak to family or friends every day.	5 points
I speak to family or friends three times a week.	3 points
I speak to family or friends less than once weekly.	0 points
5. I engage in personally meaningful activity daily.	5 points
I engage in personally meaningful activity one time a week.	3 points
I do not engage in any personally meaningful activity.	0 points
Social Domain Total Points	_____ ÷ 25

Physical Domain

Circle the response that best describes your behavior over the past three months.

	SCORE
1. I walk 10,000 steps daily.	5 points
I walk between 5,000 and 10,000 steps daily.	3 points
I do not walk.	0 points
2. I engage in aerobic exercise three hours a week.	5 points
I engage in aerobic exercise one hour a week.	3 points
I do not engage in aerobic exercise.	0 points
3. I garden more than one time a week during season.	5 points
I garden one time a week during season.	3 points
I do not garden.	0 points
4. I dance more than one time a week.	5 points
I dance one time a week.	3 points
I do not dance.	0 points
5. I knit more than one time a week.	5 points
I knit one time a week.	3 points
I do not knit.	0 points
Physical Domain Total Points	_____ ÷ 25

Mental Stimulation Domain

Circle the response that best describes your behavior during the past three months.

	SCORE
1. I read more than the news on a daily basis.	5 points
I read one new book a month.	3 points
I do not read.	0 points
2. I am fluent in more than one language.	5 points
I am learning a new language (including American Sign Language).	3 points
I am not learning a new language.	0 points
3. I handwrite on a daily basis.	5 points
I handwrite once a week.	3 points
I do not handwrite.	0 points
4. I travel to new places one time a week.	5 points
I travel to new places one time a month.	3 points
I do not travel to new places.	0 points
5. I play a musical instrument.	5 points
I am learning to play a new musical instrument.	3 points
I do not play a musical instrument.	0 points
6. I listen to classical music on a daily basis.	5 points
I listen to classical music once a week.	3 points
I do not listen to classical music.	0 points

7. I play board games or other cognitive games daily.   5 points

I play board games or other cognitive games
once weekly.   3 points

I do not play board games or cognitive games.   0 points

Mental Stimulation Domain Total Points   _____ ÷ 35

Spiritual Domain

Circle the response that best describes your behavior during the past three months.

	SCORE
1. I pray on a daily basis.	5 points
I pray one time a week.	3 points
I do not pray.	0 points
2. I meditate on a daily basis.	5 points
I meditate one time a week.	3 points
I do not meditate.	0 points
3. I engage in relaxation procedures daily.	5 points
I engage in relaxation procedures one time a week.	3 points
I do not engage in relaxation procedures.	0 points
4. I get enough sleep daily to feel rested and energetic.	5 points
I get enough sleep daily to feel somewhat rested and energetic.	3 points
I do not sleep enough to feel rested or energetic.	0 points

5. I attend a formalized place of worship weekly.   5 points

    I attend a formalized place of worship monthly.   3 points

    I do not attend a formalized place of worship.   0 points

Spiritual Domain Total Points   _____ ÷ **25**

Nutritional Domain

Circle the response that best describes your behavior during the past three months.

	SCORE
1. I eat several ounces of salmon two or more times a week.	5 points
I eat salmon, herring, mackerel, sardines, or tuna one time a week.	3 points
I do not eat fish.	0 points
2. I eat two cups of vegetables and fruits every day.	5 points
I eat two cups of vegetables and fruits one time a week.	3 points
I do not eat vegetables and fruits.	0 points
3. I drink one 4- to 6-ounce glass of red wine or grape juice daily.	5 points
I drink one 4- to 6-ounce glass of red wine or grape juice weekly.	3 points
I do not consume red wine or grape juice regularly.	0 points

4. I eat two meals with utensils daily.   5 points

   I eat one meal with utensils daily.   3 points

   I do not use utensils on a daily basis.   0 points

5. I eat walnuts or almonds several times a week.   5 points

   I eat walnuts once or twice a month.   3 points

   I do not eat walnuts.   0 points

6. I consume 80 percent of the portions provided me

     as a rule.   5 points

   I consume 100 percent of the food on my plate.   3 points

   I tend to overeat regardless of portion size.   0 points

Nutritional Domain Total Points   _____ ÷ 30

What Your Score Means

You may use the following guide to interpret your scores:

100–90: Great job! Maintain your lifestyle approach.

89–80: Good job! Make a few changes to improve your lifestyle.

79–70: Average. Consider making changes in several domains.

69–60: Poor. Significant change is needed in several domains.

59–50: Help! Reassess the importance of your life story and attempt to make one small change in your lifestyle at a time.

Do not be concerned if you score poorly at first. This is probably the first time you have considered your own brain health! You will notice improvement if you remain loyal to your brain health lifestyle!

Calculate and Interpret Your Scores

1. To derive your quarterly brain health score for each domain, add the scores of your circled responses and insert the total score into the formula listed for each one.
2. To derive your quarterly total brain health score, add the total scores for each domain, divide by 140, and then multiply by 100.
3. To derive an annual brain health score by domain, add the four scores of each domain and apply that score to the formula listed for the annual brain health score for that particular domain.

For example, here's how you would obtain an annual brain health score for the physical domain:

Total score for each quarter $\div$ 100 $\times$ 100 = _____

4. To derive a grand total for overall brain health for the year: add the five annual brain health scores together, divide by 560, and multiply by 100:

Grand Total = (five annual brain health scores) $\div$ 560
= _____ $\times$ 100 = _____

Date	SOCIAL	PHYSICAL	MENTAL	SPIRITUAL	NUTRITIONAL
Baseline Score	___ ÷ 25 = ___ ___ × 100 = ___	___ ÷ 25 = ___ ___ × 100 = ___	___ ÷ 35 = ___ ___ × 100 = ___	___ ÷ 25 = ___ ___ × 100 = ___	___ ÷ 30 = ___ ___ × 100 = ___
First Quarter	___ ÷ 25 = ___ ___ × 100 = ___	___ ÷ 25 = ___ ___ × 100 = ___	___ ÷ 35 = ___ ___ × 100 = ___	___ ÷ 25 = ___ ___ × 100 = ___	___ ÷ 30 = ___ ___ × 100 = ___
Second Quarter	___ ÷ 25 = ___ ___ × 100 = ___	___ ÷ 25 = ___ ___ × 100 = ___	___ ÷ 35 = ___ ___ × 100 = ___	___ ÷ 25 = ___ ___ × 100 = ___	___ ÷ 30 = ___ ___ × 100 = ___
Third Quarter	___ ÷ 25 = ___ ___ × 100 = ___	___ ÷ 25 = ___ ___ × 100 = ___	___ ÷ 35 = ___ ___ × 100 = ___	___ ÷ 25 = ___ ___ × 100 = ___	___ ÷ 30 = ___ ___ × 100 = ___
Fourth Quarter	___ ÷ 25 = ___ ___ × 100 = ___	___ ÷ 25 = ___ ___ × 100 = ___	___ ÷ 35 = ___ ___ × 100 = ___	___ ÷ 25 = ___ ___ × 100 = ___	___ ÷ 30 = ___ ___ × 100 = ___
Annual Brain Health Score	___ ÷ 100 = ___ ___ × 100 = ___	___ ÷ 100 = ___ ___ × 100 = ___	___ ÷ 140 = ___ ___ × 100 = ___	___ ÷ 100 = ___ ___ × 100 = ___	___ ÷ 120 = ___ ___ × 100 = ___

1

THE IMPORTANCE
OF BRAIN HEALTH

*Brain health and indeed the human brain is now securely positioned on
the radar screen of the American psyche.*

◉

The belief that a proactive approach can help to reduce the
risk of brain disease is the core principle of the brain health
movement. While the focus of this book and my career is brain
health, there remains a need to understand the consequences of
brain disease. It is from this understanding of the devastation
caused by brain disease that a strong energy to learn about and
implement brain health emerges, not out of fear, but out of a
motivation to build and preserve access to our own life story.

When thinking about brain health, we often think about
brain disease. This makes sense, as disease in general has tradi-
tionally been the focus of our medical training and approach to
health care. "Brain disease" refers to an array of conditions that
negatively affect the function of the brain. Examples range from
progressive neurodegenerative diseases, such as Alzheimer's,

Parkinson's, and Lewy body dementia, to mental illnesses, such as depression, anxiety, bipolar disorder, schizophrenia, pervasive developmental disorders, and substance abuse, to trauma, such as closed head injury. Each of these conditions, and hundreds of others, impacts the structure and function of the brain, resulting in cognitive, emotional, and functional decline for the person. Such conditions and diseases also result in significant disruption of the family system and place a tremendous emotional and practical toll on the caregiver. Because the brain is so complex and we know so little about it, our interventions are symptom-based, not curative. When considering the brain, we tend to rely on the medical approach to the human brain that overly emphasizes disease, but we should strive to take on another perspective with an eye toward brain health, development, and growth rather than relying on reactive, quick, and invasive procedures only. Brain health is proactive and lifelong, with nothing quick about it. It's a lifestyle.

For many years we have believed that the brain is a fixed and rigid entity that has a limited window of opportunity to develop, the "critical period of brain development." Traditional thinking taught us that this critical period occurred early in life and new skill development could not happen beyond that time. Similarly, the ideas that brain disease is inevitable with advanced age and that once the brain is damaged it cannot be treated or healed were generally accepted. With our new understanding of the human brain, we have begun to challenge these ideas, and the new concept of brain health maintains that a proactive approach can be implemented at the earliest period of life and followed across the entire life span. Brain health further maintains the belief that we can shape our brains for health by exposing ourselves to a specific type of environment and by engaging in specific activities as often as possible.

DEFINING DEMENTIA

Dementia is a clinical condition characterized by decline in overall intelligence relative to premorbid intellect, memory loss, personality change, and functional loss. There are nearly one hundred causes of dementia, and 95 percent of the causes of dementia are irreversible. Examples of the causes of dementia include Alzheimer's, Parkinson's, substance abuse, tumor, head injury, multiple strokes, and Lewy body. Most, though not all, types of dementia manifest in later life beyond age sixty-five. Examples of reversible causes of dementia include thyroid disorder, vitamin deficiency such as B_{12} deficiency, and depression.

Alzheimer's disease is a progressive neurodegenerative disorder, the number one cause of dementia in the United States, accounting for 50 to 70 percent of all dementias, and is often used as the model of brain disease. The disease strikes specific regions of the brain and manifests in a predictable pattern of forgetfulness, loss of appreciation of space, personality change, and other deficits in thinking and function.

As a progressive disease, the course of Alzheimer's lasts on average ten or more years and cannot be reversed. Unfortunately, this horrific disease is the leading cause of dementia in the United States, presently affecting nearly five million persons, and is a major cause of dementia internationally. The number of Alzheimer's cases in the United States will increase to a staggering fifteen million or more by the middle of this century. Indeed, the United States presently spends over one hundred billion dollars annually on direct care of Alzheimer's, and corporate America loses over thirty billion dollars annually, as the employees, who are also caregivers of parents or loved ones with Alzheimer's or dementia, miss work and develop physical and mental illness themselves.

Alzheimer's disease is a deeply personal catastrophe that robs a family of their personal connection. For me, the ultimate question is, what is the dollar amount for the fact that somebody's father or grandmother has not been able to communicate with his or her grandchild during the past decade?

The essence of this question drives the motivation for my work in the area of brain health. There can be no greater loss than the inability to connect with one's own identity and further connect with the loved ones in our lives. It is the precise reality of the husband who entered my office so many years ago in a deep depression because he could no longer connect with his wife, who was suffering from dementia, and wanted her back with him.

Alzheimer's and other brain diseases are a fact of life and an unfortunate reality for too many families. Brain disease, like brain health, does not discriminate; it unites us in a common cause regardless of background. Our energy and resources are committed to finding cures for these diseases, but our incomplete understanding of the human brain most likely means a cure for dementia is not near. However, we can and should consider the behaviors and activities that relate to brain health as a viable and necessary path to follow now to forestall or reduce the risk of brain disease.

DEGENERATIVE AND OTHER TYPES OF MEMORY LOSS

Brain dysfunction and disease can be caused in many ways. We have discussed dementia as a description of predominantly progressive forms of brain dysfunction. However, there are many other etiologies for brain dysfunction that may not be irreversible. In human brain function, so many processes need to be in balance or atypical or abnormal thinking and behavior can result. As a clinician, I have seen cognitive or thinking problems result from high and low blood pressure, urinary tract infection, medication side effect, lack of sleep, too much coffee or other stimulant, anxiety, stress, hormonal imbalance, and sugar imbalance. These and other everyday occurrences can affect a person's thinking and mood regardless of age.

It is quite common for a person in his or her fifties to begin noticing problems with memory or an inability to find an appropriate word or name as easily as in the past. For some, this may be alarming and suggest onset of a disease such as Alzheimer's. Indeed, I am often asked if I believe this represents Alzheimer's. In most cases, such slips of the tongue, temporary forgetfulness, or misplacement of objects are not disease-based. Rather, these cognitive hiccups most likely reflect stress caused by trying to do too much all at once, hormonal changes that occur naturally around the fifties, and perhaps mood fluctuations related to changes in life circumstances. But to remove any question or doubt about the severity of the problem, I recommend doing a neuropsychological assessment at any respected academic medical center.

You can always have an annual neuropsychological examination beginning in the middle fifties to monitor your memory and other cognitive functions, but dementia is quite rare at this age. The diagnosis that one does not have a degenerative dementia is good news, but it does not help with the fact that memory problems can still be frustrating. It is important to speak to your doctor about change-of-life issues, as hormonal imbalance is real, and it can cause both mood and memory problems. And it is not only those in their mid-forties and fifties who understand the power of hormonal changes. Teenage brains are notorious for distractibility, inattention, impulsivity, and downright "goofiness." Hormonal changes are a fact of the teenage brain and underlie the behavioral and cognitive changes that also can be seen at this time of life.

You can also take a personal assessment of your stress level and be honest with the idea that you may be doing too much and going too fast. Stress increases hormonal activity that can be damaging to the structural and functional capacity of the brain, particularly if the stress is severe and sustained. Animal studies demonstrate that chronic stress and overstimulation cause brain dysfunction and structural changes in the hippocampus (see Chapter 2), the part of the brain critical to new learning. On a more moderate level, stress can cause depression and anxiety, both of which alter our neurochemistry and can interfere with information processing. You should also take note of how much sleep you are getting a night. Brain functions can be affected by your sleeping patterns. Without deep sleep and dream sleep, otherwise known as REM (rapid eye movement) sleep, the brain will not process information efficiently. Increased stress and reduced rest can certainly result in cognitive mistakes, forgetfulness, mood disorder, and frustration.

Changes occur to all parts of our body as we get older, and the brain is certainly not excluded from this reality. The main message of this book is to know about your brain and to care for it for life. Hopefully, the care begins well before age fifty-five, but no age is too late to start. Lifestyle modification can be very helpful to easing the mental lapses, dysnomia (inability to name things), and misplacement of objects. You will find that writing things down can be an effective strategy for your recall. By writing things down, we provide cues and prompts that help our brains to more easily locate the information to be retrieved. The reason is that with healthy aging, the hippocampus continues to encode information fine. Our brains simply have more difficulty retrieving information, and we therefore can benefit from cues that get us to the material our brain has already encoded. Writing things down turns a free recall task into a more simple recognition memory task.

This type of normal memory change is quite different from disease such as Alzheimer's, which prevents the brain from encoding new information and in which cues will not provide any benefit. That is because dementia caused by Alzheimer's erodes the hippocampus, the encoding system for the brain, while changes typical of advanced age alone do not. Indeed studies have shown that healthy seventy- and eighty-year-old persons will perform as well as thirty-year-old persons on tests of recognition memory. One cannot recognize something unless it has been encoded, which requires a healthy hippocampus.

RAISING AWARENESS FOR BRAIN HEALTH

The human brain has always been a mysterious, misunderstood, and neglected part of the human being. Study and interest in the brain has generally taken a traditional academic approach that does not permit personalization or consumption by the general public. This is a major problem for those of us who believe all humans need to understand the basics of their brain to achieve success with promoting brain health. With the advent of new, more sensitive neuroimaging technology, our understanding of the human brain has increased and changed. We now know the human brain has "plasticity," which means it is dynamic, constantly reorganizing, and malleable—capable of being shaped structurally and functionally by the environment. This deviates from our traditional view of the human brain as a rigid and fixed system not capable of developing much beyond childhood.

It is this new thinking about the human brain that permits a new applied practice for health in both the personal and societal approach to the brain. A brain that can be shaped by environment can be shaped for health and health promotion across the life span. The key is to learn and apply those behaviors or activities that maximize brain health on a personal level. In addition, major sectors of society, including education, business, health care, religion, and nutrition, have begun to integrate our new understanding of the human brain into their particular activity for the consumer.

In order to raise awareness for brain health, grocery stores could begin labeling their products with brain icons for foods that are known to promote brain health, and the same is true for our restaurants. Schools could plan curricula on the human brain at the earliest of ages, and Head Start and baby wellness programs should be enriched with brain health information. Corporations could include brain health as part of every employee orientation and wellness program, and our nation's prevention and wellness programs need to include brain health. It is from the personal and larger societal recognition of new brain research that a not-so-quiet revolution on brain health has emerged in the United States and internationally.

Today more of the general public is interested in the human brain, how it operates, and how it can be shaped for health. The human brain is no longer the domain of academia or medicine. Indeed, the general public has now taken some ownership of this part of their body, and there is great excitement and motivation to learn about what behaviors can help to shape a healthy brain. As the general public gets more involved in learning about the human brain, people are understanding that health of the brain is a very personal issue. This is particularly true when we consider that our brain contains our life story and that a significant concern for baby boomers is the loss of our memory (life story) as we get older. Brain health is no longer a technical or academic story. Rather, the general public has made it a highly personal priority to be integrated into daily lifestyle for health.

The human brain contains our very identity, catalog of memories, ability to communicate, and life story. A cruel reality is that brain disease can rob the brain of one's life story and even disconnect one's own identity and relationships with family members. It is from this personal devastation that a dedication to promotion of brain health becomes paramount. Indeed, a lifelong and proactive pursuit of brain health is critical to each person, because everyone has a life story that needs to be shared. My work and this book are dedicated to educating each person on the basics of his or her brain and to promoting a brain health lifestyle that can help maximize access to one's life story at any age.

We are indeed undergoing a not-so-quiet revolution about the human brain and brain health. The concept of brain health is now discussed in major sectors of society, including personal development, health care, business, media, and even religion. It is quite common to see information on brain health in major news outlets, popular magazines, peer-reviewed medical journals, business periodicals, new business start-ups that apply product and educational information on brain health to the general public, retail, and even television programming. This is good news because it indicates a cultural shift in which the United States and other nations are prepared and willing to begin the process of integrating brain health into our language and, more important, into our daily health regimen.

Personalizing Brain Health

One of the great paradoxes of our time is the fact that the human brain is the single greatest, most magnificent system ever designed in the history of the universe! Simultaneously, most Americans do not know the basics of their own brain, and they cannot be expected to take care of their brain. The same is most likely true of nearly everyone around the world. A 2006 survey of Americans on brain health sponsored by MetLife Foundation and the American Society on Aging (asaging .org) found only 3 percent identified brain health as a leading health topic. More promising, the same survey found a majority (88 percent) believe they can keep their brains fit, and nearly 90 percent believe regular checkups for their brain are important. Americans also demonstrate a decent understanding of what activities are considered good for brain health. In order for our nation and nations around the globe to be enlightened about brain health, we need to do a better job educating all citizens about the human brain, and I believe this education should begin early in life. The story of your brain needs to be a personal one!

As one example of health promotion that is personal, the United States has done a good job educating the public about the importance of cardiac, or heart, health. We decided to prioritize heart health because many of our loved ones have cardiac illness, and cardiac illness represents a primary cause of death. Interestingly, over the past decade, research indicates that while cardiac illness remains a leading cause of death, inroads have been made to slow the rate of cardiac-caused premature death.

Our culture has also adopted a great awareness and, in some sense, a fondness for the heart as a favorite organ in our body. Like the ancient Egyptians, we have a belief that our being revolves around the heart. Our language contains many statements that give the heart meaning it really does not deserve. For example, statements such as "I love you with all my heart," "the Steelers played their hearts out," and "you broke my heart" suggest our heart has the capacity for emotion or feelings. Indeed, the human heart is a pump that perfuses blood throughout the body. It has no capacity to feel emotions like love, have thoughts, or direct motor skills. All of the emotions and thoughts that we relate to the heart are really owned by the brain. In this regard, our brains have not been treated fairly, and I believe it is time we begin to show our brain a little love and the attention it deserves. Similar to the sense of urgency we feel about cardiac health because we lose so many of our loved ones prematurely due to heart disease, we must be vigilant to the fact that we are also losing many of our loved ones to Alzheimer's, stroke, Parkinson's, and other diseases of the brain.

Educating Others About the Benefits of a Healthy Brain

We have persistent educational campaigns to teach the public about behaviors that promote cardiac health. Consider the relatively recent introduction of aerobic centers, exercise clubs, and television programs on exercise. Grocery stores and our nation's restaurants have sections dedicated to heart-healthy foods. There are even icons of red hearts that identify for the consumer those foods that promote heart health. These are concrete efforts that help consumers live heart-healthy lifestyles. The message of heart health is not academic or clinical; it is personal.

We are so lucky to be alive at this period in our nation's history. We have an unprecedented opportunity to be part of a societal shift toward brain health that will likely lead to an unleashing of human potential and a reduction in brain disease. Some of our advances may occur in the development of traditional medical interventions such as a vaccine or new medication therapy. Gene therapy and stem cell research, which uses our own stem cells to combat disease, may offer an entirely new frontier of treatment or prevention options. Another major advancement is a new national priority on the human brain that declares our desire to address the fact that we are losing many of our family members to brain disease.

The United States and other countries can foster a new and enlightened outlook on brain health by implementing lifelong educational programs on the basics of the human brain. Schools can integrate basic curriculum on the human brain and brain health promotion at the earliest ages. Libraries can be reintroduced as community brain health centers, where basic education and actual implementation of brain health lifestyle programs can be offered. Preventative programs, both publicly and privately based, can adopt and help to pay for a brain health lifestyle for all of us, and brain health centers that recognize and offer research-based activities for the consumer can emerge. Our grocery stores and restaurants can begin the process of identifying for the consumer foods that have brain-health-promoting effects. New businesses and retail outlets that cater to the vitality of the human brain and our cognitive and emotional abilities will continue to emerge.

A nation that prioritizes brain health understands that a life-long and proactive lifestyle is needed. Individuals must educate themselves about their own brain and begin to make the behavioral changes necessary to develop as healthy a brain as possible. Businesses, schools, churches, the media, and health care systems can begin to promote brain health in their own specialized ways, and our daily language will reflect a society that embraces the importance of caring for our brains. Ultimately, however, the desire for education on the basics of the human brain and desire to change behavior toward a proactive and lifelong brain health lifestyle begins with the individual.

2

How Your
Brain Works

There will never be anything developed by mankind that approximates
the power and efficiency of the human brain.

◉

We know that the human brain is a wonderfully complex system that permits our every thought, emotion, and movement. It is very important for you to learn about the basics of your brain and how your brain actually works to grasp the importance of the brain health lifestyle. This chapter is dedicated to helping you understand how your own brain works and how you really have an important role in being able to shape your own brain for health.

Parts of the Brain

The study of the human brain can be a very intimidating undertaking, and this might actually keep some from even trying to learn. I want you to realize that your brain is really about who you are. If you can personalize this brilliant system that sits within your skull, you can begin the process of learning about you. There are actually some easy methods to learn about the structures and functions of your brain: I teach the basics of the brain using some simple techniques that organize the brain into different sections. This typically makes the learning quite simple and interesting. Give it a try and learn something new about yourself.

The first learning technique is to think of the brain divided into a "top-down" orientation, with cortex at the top and the subcortex at the bottom. While these two regions of the brain are distinct, each with specific responsibilities, they are also integrated, helping the brain to operate like a symphony.

Cortex

Your brain weighs two to four pounds and is made up of gray matter and white matter. The gray matter tends to be contained in an area of your brain called the *cortex*, a word that translates to "bark of a tree." Your cortex (see Figure 2.1) is a convoluted mass of cells with folds and flaps that sits snug within your skull. The white matter is situated more deeply in the brain, beneath the cortex, and helps to bridge or connect different regions of the brain. White matter helps to propel information and to insulate cells and nerve tracts.

It developed from the back to the front, meaning the front part of your cortex is the most recent member or region of your

FIGURE 2.1 THE CEREBRAL CORTEX

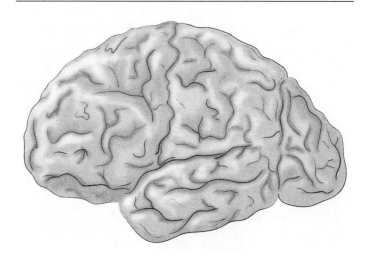

brain to develop, evolutionally speaking. The cortex is primarily responsible for your most complex thinking abilities, including memory, language, planning, concept formation, problem solving, spatial representation, auditory and visual processing, mood, and personality. Processing in the cortex tends to be conscious and intentional. For example, the cortex is responsible for your reading this book at this very moment—your intent to educate yourself about brain health is driven by your cortex.

The cortex is generally organized by four primary regions, or lobes: the frontal, temporal, parietal, and occipital (see Figure 2.2). Each of these four lobes has specific behaviors and functions primary to its region. For example, the frontal lobes are

Figure 2.2 The Four Lobes of the Brain

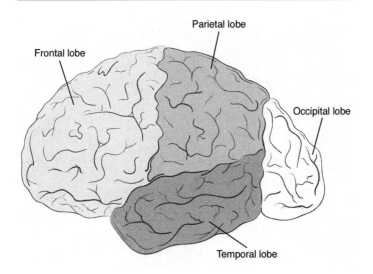

also known as the *executive system* since they help execute behavior, organize behavior, plan, conceptualize, maintain cognitive flexibility, and stabilize mood. Your personality is thought to reside in the frontal region of your brain. Your temporal lobes are the site of your auditory brain, memory and new learning, language, and perhaps religiosity. Your parietal lobes help you with orientation to space, memory, reading and writing, mathematics, and appreciation of left versus right. Finally, your occipital lobes help you to see, discriminate what you see, and perceive.

Subcortex

Sitting just under the cortex and on top of the ascending brain stem are a number of smaller and generally more primitive structures (relative to the cortex) known as the *subcortex*. Your subcortex primarily processes rote skills and procedures. Some, if not most, of the processing conducted in the subcortex is subconscious. Activities such as driving, dressing, typing, and most other routine tasks involve multiple rote procedures that are conducted at a subconscious level. Your subcortex and cortex are distinct regions of the brain, but they do not sit in isolation of one another. In fact, there are numerous connections between these two important brain regions. The brain operates as a symphony, with numerous and distinct regions harmonizing perfectly as one unit.

Left and Right Hemispheres

The second learning technique divides the brain "left to right," appreciating that the brain is comprised of two distinct yet integrated hemispheres we call the *dominant* and *non-dominant* sides of the brain. We refer to these sides as *hemispheres*, and you have a left hemisphere and a right hemisphere (see Figure 2.3). Each hemisphere is connected by a bridge known as the *corpus callosum*. As you will learn in this section, each hemisphere has some distinct, yet not necessarily mutually exclusive, responsibilities.

Interestingly, your behaviors and functions are related primarily to one of these two hemispheres. For example, most of

FIGURE 2.3 THE HEMISPHERES OF THE BRAIN

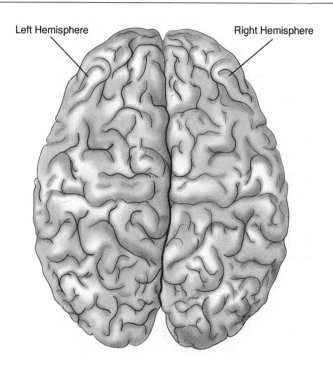

Left Hemisphere   Right Hemisphere

us—and nearly all right-handers—have language distributed primarily in the left hemisphere. We refer to the hemisphere in which language is based as the dominant hemisphere as a sign of our respect for the importance of language. Left-handers with a parent who is left-handed, a relatively rare phenomenon, have a higher probability than right-handers of having language functioning distributed primarily in the right hemisphere. They would be right-hemisphere dominant.

Your dominant hemisphere—left for most of us—also processes details, is task-oriented, logical, analytical, and sequences information. Most of Western civilization is built around the left hemisphere, as our classrooms are set up in rows and columns of chairs, and our cities tend to have tall buildings in rows and columns. We tend to focus more on the detail and less on the gestalt. Your non-dominant hemisphere helps you process non-language information, such as size, shapes, sounds, and space. Your ability to navigate in space, locate your car in a parking garage, or get home from a walk is an example of non-dominant function. Likewise, your ability to appreciate distinct sounds, such as a baby's cry or a fire alarm, tends to be a process of the non-dominant hemisphere.

Your two hemispheres are connected by a bridge of cells referred to as the *corpus callosum*. Information crosses from one side of your brain to the other over the corpus callosum, and this is a critical part of your brain's ability to remain so functional despite its many complex operations on a daily basis. Interestingly, the female brain is thought to have a larger corpus callosum, which underscores the notion that female brains process information differently from male brains. Females tend to utilize both sides of their brains more to process than men, who tend to rely primarily on one side, the dominant hemisphere. It is probably not coincidental that audiences across the nation always respond with the same answer to my question, "In what area of a common behavior do men and women struggle with each other on a daily basis?" The answer is communication, which you'll learn more about in the chapters ahead.

Neurons

The operation and function of your brain is ultimately conducted by the millions of brain cells we refer to as *neurons*. A neuron (see Figure 2.4) contains a cell body sometimes referred to as a *soma*, a long arm extending out from the cell body referred to as an *axon*, and branchlike figures called *dendrites* that extend out into the brain environment seeking new information to relay back to the cell body.

Indeed, information from the cell body travels down the axon into the surrounding brain, while information from the environment is gathered by the dendrites and brought back to the cell body. This ongoing exchange of information by the brain is why we refer to it as the *central information processing system*.

We are taught that our brains contain millions of brain cells and that each neuron can communicate with another ten thousand neurons. Interestingly, one neuron never touches another neuron, but two cells may communicate via chemicals, and this chemical marriage is called a *synapse*. The more synaptic connections you develop over your life span, the healthier your brain may be, because it is building up *brain reserve*. Brain reserve, as you will learn, may have the ability to delay the onset of neurodegenerative diseases such as Alzheimer's.

The miracle is that your brain is dynamic and continues to be shaped and to develop. It has *plasticity*. As such, there is no finite capacity or limitation. In this way, your brain is very distinct and actually much superior to the fanciest of all computers because computers will always have built-in limitations and

FIGURE 2.4 A NEURON

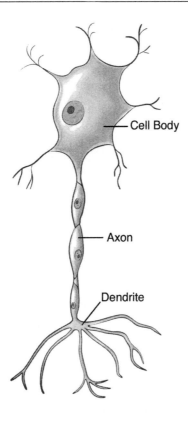

Cell Body

Axon

Dendrite

finite capacity. Your dynamic brain is shaped by environmental input across your life span, beginning in the womb. There really is no critical period of brain development, unless one considers life itself to be the measure. As you will learn in the next section, the type of environmental input your brain receives can make a

difference regarding the health of your brain. You do have some
control, and this is great news!

Hippocampus

When I give lectures to the public, I always want my audience
to personalize the message. This story is, after all, about you and
your brain. It really does not get any more personal. Learning
about oneself can be fun and challenging. There is one part
of your brain that I emphasize because this structure, the *hippocampus*, is so critical to you and your life story. A hippocampus (see Figure 2.5) sits in the middle of each of your temporal
lobes, which lie under your temples on each side of your head.

Your hippocampus, or hippocampi, for plural, as you have
one in each hemisphere, takes new information in and maintains the information in a type of working buffer. If you believe
the information is important and you need to store the information for an extended period of time, your hippocampus will
transition the information to a specific area of your cortex. This
process is not random, but rather very sophisticated, as the process of storage seems to be stimulus-based. That is, if you are
learning information that is visual, your hippocampus will help
store that information permanently in the visual cortex of the
brain. The same process is thought to occur for the other four
types of sensory input: sound, touch, taste, and smell.

Your hippocampi represent your vital learning and encoding structures, thereby helping you to build your life story and
maintain your personal memories. Alzheimer's disease, as men-

FIGURE 2.5 THE HIPPOCAMPUS

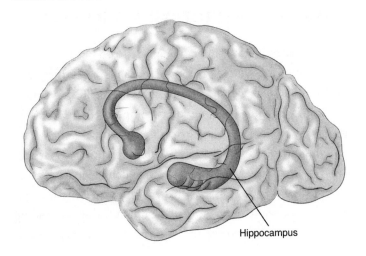

Hippocampus

tioned in the previous chapter, is a leading cause of dementia, and the disease destroys very early the hippocampi of the brain. As a result, those afflicted with this terrible brain disease cannot learn new information, and they typically will repeat statements. As you will learn in the next section, your hippocampi are critical structures to brain health. Recent research suggests your hippocampi have tremendous ability, including new brain cell development referred to as *neurogenesis.*

Environmental Effects on Brain Plasticity and Reserve

We now believe that the human brain is shaped by our environment. This means that our brain will respond to everything that we do and all that is going on around us. Something as simple as a television show or a hug, or as complicated as screaming at someone or experiencing loss and grief affects the structure and function of our brain. This wonderfully intricate marriage between environment and brain function defines neural plasticity and enables us to consider what environmental input might be best to promote our own brain health. Your understanding of this simple fact and the power of neural plasticity permits you to engage in a proactive effort to shape your own brain across your life span.

Every day we have experiences that can teach us about the function of our brain and how environment and our brain have an important and ongoing relationship. I often say that the chemistry of our brains is altered all the time, but not with pills, syringes, or liquids. Instead, words may be the single greatest neurochemical activator, and messages provided to us by our parents have a particularly long-term effect. Other environmental stimuli, such as temperature, touch from another, pain, imagery on television or the movies, emotional events, news, victory and defeat, loss, and many others affect our mood and disposition, a result of neurochemical change. Such change then typically leads to behavioral change, and this is how we lead our lives. In short, environment shapes our neurophysiology and behavior every day.

It is important you learn about the power of your brain and how it can be shaped and nurtured over the course of your life. We refer to the dynamic, constantly reorganizing, and malleable nature of your brain as *brain plasticity*. Understand that your brain is not a rigid or static system with a limited capacity or finite critical period for development. The power of brain plasticity permits you to implement a lifelong and proactive program to grow and promote your own brain health.

Animal Brain Research: How the Environment Affects the Brain

To better understand why brain plasticity is important to you, we can look to some basic findings of animal brain research. In the 1950s, research was conducted to investigate whether environment had any effect on the structure and function of the animal brain. Researchers designed a study with rodents raised in two distinct environments: an "enriched" environment versus an "unenriched" environment. Rodents were raised in one of these two environments, and then their brains were analyzed and compared at autopsy. Results yielded significant differences in the brains of these rodents. Specifically, rodents raised in an enriched environment had a larger cortex, more cellular connections, called *synapses*, that lead to brain reserve, and developed new brain cells, called *neurogenesis*, in the hippocampus, the structure critical to new learning and memory.

I became interested in this work, and I wanted to know how researchers defined an enriched environment. My review of this work suggests three factors were critical to the enriched environment: *socialization* (animals had to have other animals of their own kind in the environment); *physical activity* (animals had a running wheel to exercise on); and *mental stimulation* (there were toys in the environment animals could play and interact with). Animals raised in unenriched environments were raised in isolation, had no running wheel, and had no toys to play with. While this research offered highly significant and important findings regarding the effects of the environment on brain structure in the animal, the critical issue of whether the same findings could be established for humans remained unknown.

When thinking about a proactive brain health lifestyle, I believe the three critical factors of the enriched environment found in the animal studies are equally important to humans. Plenty of research supports the role of socialization, physical activity, and mental stimulation in reducing the risk of dementia in humans. However, the human organism is more complex than rodents and is stimulated by environmental input that is also more complex in nature. As you will learn in later chapters, my brain health lifestyle recognizes the complexity of the human brain by including two new factors, nutrition and spirituality, in addition to the three factors established from the animal literature.

How Environment Affects the Human Brain

It was not until the late nineties that a landmark study discovered that the human brain has the ability to generate new brain cells. This study was a threshold moment for our species, as it confronted traditional thought that the human brain was a rigid system with no ability to regenerate. We had always believed the brain was born with all of its brain cells, that the human brain lost brain cells on a daily basis, and that our brains did not replace the lost cells with new ones. The study also indicated that the new brain cells were generated in the human hippocampus, analogous in animals to an area neurogenesis was found in the animal brain. Today, research is ongoing to determine if neurogenesis occurs in other regions of the human brain or if it is specific to the hippocampus.

New brain cell development is one outcome of a brain with plasticity. Remember, plasticity refers to a brain that is dynamic, constantly reorganizing, and malleable. The human brain, therefore, is now thought to possess the same type of neural plasticity as the rodent brain. Interestingly, the animal studies were conducted on rodents across their life span with an equivalent human age of seventy or eighty. A human brain that generates new brain cells mandates a curiosity of how this wonderful adaptive ability occurs. We can return to the animal studies to derive some answers to this question. The enriched environment led to new brain cell development in the hippocampus of the animal. The three critical factors important to the enriched environment in this study included socialization, physical activity, and mental stimulation. Therefore, it makes sense to ask if the human brain is similarly affected by environment and if the enriched environment promotes positive brain changes in the human.

As you will read in the next chapter, there is good reason to believe that the human brain benefits from a novel and complex environment. Similar to the enriched environment discussed in the animal research above, novelty and complexity infers stimulation that demands more of the human cerebral cortex and increases the potential for development of brain reserve. Stimuli that are novel and complex require the cortex to be engaged, as the brain has either not been exposed to the information before or it has not mastered the information. In contrast, passive, rote talents or overlearned information rely more on the subcortex and are not thought to be as brain health promoting. It is also important to know that the first potential enriched environment is the womb and that the type of environment you expose your brain to will have consequences your entire life. The miracle of brain plasticity does not end at a particular age. Indeed, the human brain probably does not know its chronological age and will demand and benefit from enriched environments at every age. The major point of this section is that you are strongly encouraged and empowered to expose your brain to the novel and complex every day regardless of your age!

Enhancing Brain Reserve

Brain reserve is a well-known concept that refers to a buildup of brain cell connections that serves to assist the brain in the battle against neurodegenerative diseases. To better understand brain reserve, consider the following simple analogy that I use in my lectures on the human brain. Imagine flying in an airplane nearly a thousand feet above the ground. As you peer out your window down at the ground, you will see two very distinct scenes. The first scene is a jungle where there are so many trees you cannot see the ground. The second scene is an island with one palm tree blowing slowly in the wind. You want your brain to be like the jungle, the lush foliage symbolizing a tremendous number of synaptic connections. This is referred to as *synaptic density* and is a direct measure of brain reserve. You do not want your brain to look like the island with one palm tree. The reason is also simple. Think of Alzheimer's or other types of dementia or brain disease as a weed-whacker: the disease will invade the brain and begin to cut down the neurons and synaptic connections. This occurs just like a weed-whacker cutting through the weeds around your house. If your brain looks like a jungle, filled with synaptic connections, it will take Alzheimer's or another brain disease a long time to show its ugly clinical face. However, if your brain looks like the island with one palm tree, the clinical signs of Alzheimer's will manifest quickly because there is no reserve to fight it off.

Indeed, some research has shown that even though brains are diagnosed with Alzheimer's at autopsy due to the presence of neuropathological markers such as tangles and plaques, a significant number of these persons never demonstrated the clinical aspects of the disease in life. This is explained one way using the brain reserve concept. Perhaps people who never manifested Alzheimer's in life, even though they had the neuropathologic characteristics in their brain at autopsy, had built up brain reserve to fight off or delay the onset of the disease.

The power of brain reserve to stave off the effects of Alzheimer's is further supported by findings that relate higher education and occupational levels to lower risk of Alzheimer's. For those with high education or occupation levels who do manifest Alzheimer's, their disease begins to emerge later on than for those without this kind of background, and once the disease manifests, they die soon after. The theoretical reason for this is that when the disease presents clinically, it is already advanced into the final stage because the person's brain reserve had been fighting it off.

Educational settings and workplace settings are good examples of environments that can be enriched. You expose your brain to these environments frequently across over the course of your life. Each of these two environments provides the opportunity for you to engage in a novel and complex setting that promotes the development of brain reserve. To the extent that these environments or other settings become rote and passive, brain reserve will not be as developed, and the overall health benefit for your brain is not enhanced.

It is your personal challenge to expose your brain to novel and complex experiences and enriched environments on a daily basis. Studies suggest the earlier in life you begin to expose yourself to enriched environments, the greater the health benefit to your brain—even well into your late life. This finding is supported by research that demonstrates that having a higher IQ in childhood and young adulthood reveals a reduced risk of Alzheimer's and other brain health issues later in life. Language development in young adulthood also reveals a reduced risk of neuropathologic changes in the brain, while those who have passive lifestyles in their forties show an increased risk of Alzheimer's and other brain disorders later on in life.

Passive lifestyle is defined by a list of activities that do not require much in the way of cortical activation. One example on the list was television viewing, a behavior that tends to be rather mundane and nonengaging in most cases. Passivity can be thought of as using the subcortex primarily when we are engaged in routines, rote processes, and even subconscious behaviors. Active behaviors are more brain health promoting because we are stimulating our cortex with conscious and complex thinking that helps to build brain reserve. Brain health promotion is about the activation of the cortex through completion of tasks that are "complex and novel."

These findings on humans support the idea that diseases of the brain that manifest late in life may actually begin early in life. Further, these findings suggest we can become involved very early in life with a proactive lifestyle that promotes brain health and that helps to reduce the risk of Alzheimer's and related dementias later in life. It is important to prioritize a proactive lifestyle for brain health regardless of your age, to embrace the power of brain plasticity and development of brain reserve, and to have fun in the process of caring for your brain!

REVIEWING THE BRAIN BASICS

You have now accomplished something you may not have thought possible: you have learned the basics of your brain. In fact, you now know more about the human brain and yourself than the vast majority of other people. This new knowledge enables you to really appreciate the importance of a proactive brain health lifestyle because you now can understand how what you do quite literally impacts the very structures and functions of your brain. Behavioral change is most likely to occur if one personalizes the message and is told why something will help him or her. You have personalized the message, and your new knowledge of brain basics enables you to move forward fully prepared for not only understanding the brain health lifestyle but being able to apply it with great understanding.

Now that you have basic knowledge of how the brain works, you probably feel empowered and excited to learn more!

3

ADOPTING A HEALTHY BRAIN LIFESTYLE

What you do will have a consequence on your brain,
good, bad, or neutral!

◉

Long before I earned a Ph.D. in clinical psychology, I was interested in human behavior. Humans are the most fascinating animals, with all of our emotions, behaviors, and complex lifestyles. Behavior can change for a variety of reasons, and the ability of our brains to manage our thoughts, emotions, and impulses is remarkable. It is truly amazing we get along as well as we do. It has been my keen interest in human behavior that led me to study psychology and, more important, think critically about why humans do what they do and why we choose not to change behavior even if that lifestyle change can increase the quality of our lives.

We prefer daily routines with predictable outcomes and develop schedules with predictable expectations and behavioral outcomes. Structure and organization is, admittedly, very important, as chaos can break down a person, family, and even a government. Anything that can disrupt this predictable flow of behavior can be experienced as a threat and resisted. Indeed, we do not react well to change, particularly when it is unexpected. Change can cause our systems stress, leading to internal discord, interpersonal tension, and even development of physical symptoms that really represent the stress we are experiencing.

From a brain perspective, routine is interesting because it is easier for our brain to process. Habits, overlearned procedures, and talents rely on a specific region of our brain known as the subcortex, which is, as discussed in the previous chapter, a collection of small cellular structures that sit deep inside the brain just under the cortex and above the brain stem. The subcortex is sometimes referred to as the "older brain" or "more primitive brain" relative to the newer cortex. Those behaviors, rituals, skills, and procedures that tend to be processed at the subconscious level are the result of subcortical processing. Because these behaviors do not involve much conscious effort, there is a probability that this type of action is not as promoting of brain health as action that does demand ongoing conscious effort. Indeed, brain reserve, the hallmark of brain health, is most likely the result of conscious processing related to the cortex.

For those interested in brain health and leading a lifestyle that maximizes brain health, understanding the difference between active, conscious behavior and passive, subconscious behavior is critical. Promoting brain health is a conscious cortical and effortful process. Rote, passive, and subconscious behaviors, most of which are a necessary part of our life, are not as promoting of brain health. Understanding the difference between active and passive behaviors, between the conscious and subconscious, and between the complex and novel and rote processing is the first step to behavioral change—and the first step to adopting a healthy brain lifestyle!

SEEKING EXPERIENCES THAT ARE NOVEL AND COMPLEX

I am often asked if particular behaviors are good or healthy for the brain. As an example, people will ask me if the *New York Times* crossword puzzle is good for the brain. This is a good question because it tells me the person is thinking about his or her lifestyle and its potential impact on the brain. You most likely will have noted that I use the terms "novel" and "complex" to help you understand what types of behaviors or activities promote brain health. Your brain wants to be stimulated at every age, and we have already learned that the conscious behaviors that are processed by the cortex lead to a greater development of brain reserve, that which really represents brain health.

Novel means new and *complex* means hard. Ask yourself if a given behavior is complex and novel for you. If the answer is yes, then the behavior is most likely one that will be processed by the cortex and thus will help to develop brain reserve, promoting brain health. If the answer is no, the behavior is most likely rote or passive, processed by the subcortex, and therefore most likely not brain health promoting.

The reason a novel and complex behavior or activity promotes brain health is that the brain has not experienced the particular behavior. If a behavior or activity is actually new to the brain, there are very few neural circuits to facilitate the behavior. It is as if the region of the brain necessary to conduct the behavior is dormant and needs to be activated. An activity that is novel and complex is most likely one that is difficult for you, one that you do not want to do—at least at first—and one that will make you feel inferior initially. However, as the brain practices that which is considered novel and complex, it continues to develop brain cells (building of brain reserve) necessary to produce the given behavior, and over time, a talent emerges. A person will describe this transition as "I am more comfortable with this," or "I am getting the hang of this," to really describe what is happening in the brain at the cellular level. The reason the person is feeling more comfortable is that the brain is developing more neurons to facilitate his or her ability to produce the behavior. Practicing novel and complex activity results in a neurophysiological process that not only permits a smooth execution of the particular behavior (now a talent) but also leads to building brain reserve!

On the opposite end of the spectrum, we can also choose activities that are rote and passive. Indeed, much of our time is spent on activities that are rote and passive. It is human nature to do that which we are good at and comfortable with, likely in part because the rote and passive is also easier for our brains, but unfortunately these activities do not use the cortex and do not result in development of brain reserve.

Adoption and implementation of a brain health lifestyle requires you to make a conscious decision to welcome more activities that are novel and complex, to resist the passive and rote, and to realize that this will be hard and that failure will be a healthy reality. From failure will come success, and this can only occur with development of brain reserve. You've probably heard the phrase "No pain, no gain," and the same is true for engaging in novel and complex activities to promote brain health.

OVERCOME THE AUTOMATIC RESISTANCE TO CHANGE YOUR LIFESTYLE

Your understanding of how and why the novel and complex leads to brain health is a critical first step to adopting a brain health lifestyle. However, once you understand the mechanics of how brain reserve occurs through stimulation of the cortex, it is also necessary to introspect and review your current lifestyle.

It is normal for all of us to engage in a daily routine that is highly procedural, predictable, and without much that is new. It bears repeating that when we engage in such a daily routine, we are relying heavily on brain structures and functions that do not facilitate development of brain reserve. Because our daily routines are so entrenched, we are not even conscious of them for the most part; we simply act. Our ability to make our behaviors conscious and to actually try and change our daily routines is a practical but difficult means to activate our cortex and to begin the process of building brain reserve. The first step is to become conscious of what we do every day.

Think about your daily routine—it will help you identify how much rote and passive behavior you have in your life. For example, most of us probably get out of bed, make some coffee or tea, get cleaned and dressed for the day, travel to work, and engage in the daily tasks of our occupation. Most of these behaviors are done at the subconscious level because they are so habitual. To change this routine, you first must know what your routine is. You can then attempt to make some small changes, thereby creating a new set of behaviors during your day that will activate your cortex and promote development of brain reserve.

You might be surprised by what you discover, but remember, most humans are highly routinized animals by nature. The transition from the rote and passive to the novel and complex requires you to ask for each behavior, is this novel and complex for me?

Ask yourself the following questions: Can I sit at a different seat at my dinner table for the next seven days consecutively? Can I sleep on a different side of the bed for the next seven days consecutively? Can I survive moving the trash can in the kitchen? These questions are meant to have some fun, but they also raise the important point that change of routine is perhaps one of the most difficult challenges humans incur. If we cannot sleep on a different side of the bed, how are we going to be able to adopt a new diet or begin an exercise routine? These are a few simple questions that I pose to my audiences across the country to help them realize how hard behavioral change actually is. It may be the most difficult thing for us humans to accomplish, particularly if the change needs to be sustained over time. My contention is that behavioral change can occur, but we first need to personalize the message of change, and we need to know why we are changing a particular behavior.

You eventually want to fill your day with as many novel and complex activities as you can, though a good place to begin is to include one a day and build from there. This is the fundamental and personal process of building a brain health lifestyle. The goal is to build brain reserve across your life span because this process is health promoting.

Humans resist the transition from rote and passive to the novel and complex because it is hard. It places them in an uncomfortable situation, it is unpredictable, and it does not nurture the ego as failure occurs. The good news is that persistence can result in the novel and complex becoming rote, the uncomfortable becoming comfortable, the unpredictable becoming predictable, and even the development of the ego. It's a great feeling to know that you have worked hard to master a particular activity that was difficult for you in the past. Remember, the lifelong process for brain health is to continue exposing your brain to the novel and complex.

The fact that humans resist change is directly related to an increase in obesity, diabetes, and hypertension and is indirectly related to conditions such as stroke and dementia. It is well documented that lifestyle is perhaps the single greatest factor that we can control to improve not only our health but our longevity. It is lifestyle and not any health care system that contributes to health versus disease and longevity versus premature death. We can cut premature death in half if we exercise, eat healthier, and do not smoke. How can something sound so simple and yet be so hard to achieve? The answer is that humans do not like to change. It is difficult for us to change our eating habits, to engage in a consistent exercise routine, to slow down and reduce our stress, to create time for more socialization, and to engage in the novel and complex. Yet these are the five domains of the brain health lifestyle (nutrition, socialization, physical activity, mental stimulation, spirituality) that need attention and change in order to increase your chance of maintaining access to your life story!

COMMIT TO A HEALTHY BRAIN LIFESTYLE

An unfortunate reality is that unhealthy lifestyles lead to diseases like obesity, diabetes, and brain-related health problems, all of which increase the risk of stroke, dementia, and Alzheimer's as well. The good news is that these conditions can be managed and even prevented by a healthy lifestyle. Lifestyle begins with an attitude that declares, "I am committed to a life of healthy choices." You can become a champion of a proactive brain health lifestyle and actually serve as a role model to others, particularly your children and grandchildren.

We already know about several basic preventative measures to take every day for brain health, like wearing a helmet when riding a bike, wearing a seatbelt when in the car, and being cautious with activities that have the potential to cause head injuries. But, in addition to these safety tips, research shows that brain health is promoted by a lifestyle that includes stress reduction, consumption of antioxidants and omega-3 fatty acids, physical exercise, socialization, and exposure to enriched environments with the novel and complex. A conscious choice to review your current lifestyle and begin implementing change within each of these five domains to the brain health lifestyle is critical. Additionally, lifestyle is proactive, energized, and life-long. A lifestyle that promotes health will be effective at any age, but the earlier you get started, the better the outcome. Your goal should be to make the brain health lifestyle a routine in your life.

Adoption of a brain-healthy lifestyle can occur on an individual basis and on a more macro or societal basis. The individual basis is probably most important and most efficient, as you have direct control over the change. However, every nation should consider prioritizing brain health and implement policies that reinforce this priority. Now let's take a closer look at the five critical areas for brain health and what you can do to keep your brain young, fit, and sharp!

4

THE FIVE CRITICAL
AREAS OF
BRAIN HEALTH

*I have a wonderful opportunity to care for and
to shape my brain for health.*

⊙

Your brain is a highly dynamic and constantly reorganizing system capable of being shaped across your entire life
span. Similar to animals, the human brain can generate new
brain cells and respond to environmental input. Your goal is to
expose your brain to enriched environments, to the novel and
complex, and to grow your brain reserve!

As we discussed in the previous chapter, stimuli that are
considered rote and passive to your brain are most likely not as
health promoting. We learned from animal brain research that
an enriched environment has three critical components: socialization, physical activity, and mental stimulation. It makes per-
fect sense to consider these same critical factors as important

to the human brain, especially in light of research on humans suggesting their role in staving off the ravages of Alzheimer's.

In addition to these three factors, I have included two new ones that are critical to promotion of brain health. The first is spirituality, which reflects the importance of reducing stress in our lives, slowing down, and appreciating the moment. The second is nutrition, which respects the fact that what we eat literally changes the physical and functional aspects of our body and relates directly to our overall health, including brain health. Each of these five factors of my brain health lifestyle is backed up by robust research to support its effectiveness. Most important, the lifestyle needs to be integrated, comprehensive, and proactive to be most effective for health and brain health. To recap, I have proposed a lifestyle that includes the following five areas critical to brain health:

- Socialization
- Physical activity
- Mental stimulation
- Spirituality
- Nutrition

Each of these factors is necessary to your brain health lifestyle, and together they form an integrated whole for you. The five factors need to be understood as one lifestyle and not separate entities. Remember, your goal is to adopt a proactive lifestyle for brain health that increases your brain reserve through exposure to the complex and novel. As with any lifestyle program, the journey can be challenging, but your brain health lifestyle is a lifelong journey toward wholeness and will require constant personal review and change. While adopting to any lifestyle change is not easy, the goal of a healthier and more challenged brain is worthwhile.

RESEARCH-BASED APPROACH: IDENTIFYING THE FIVE CRITICAL AREAS

My healthy brain program is research-based, easily understood, and practical, as anyone can consider making changes to incorporate these activities into their own daily life. The other positive aspect of my lifestyle is that anyone can assess each of the five different lifestyle domains and understand which is a strength and which is a weakness, thereby providing a guide as to where the biggest change in behavior may need to occur. My program rests on the cognitive construct of brain reserve and the belief that neural plasticity affords the brain a wonderful opportunity to achieve health.

While my brain health lifestyle is developed from a sound understanding of brain and behavior, cognitive science, and clinical research, I realize that a practical way to apply the lifestyle is in many ways most critical—you'll find all of the practical strategies to implement this lifestyle in the chapters ahead.

The brain health program that I offer you is unique in that it is lifestyle-based, comprehensive, and integrates many different research findings into one practical approach that is easy to adopt. My brain health lifestyle was applied recently as part of a small pilot investigation with healthy independent older adults. This work was done together with Emeritus Assisted Living (www.Emeritus.com) at a campus in the Boston region. I believe we were the first to launch a prospective lifestyle study on brain health (Dr. Nussbaum's Brain Health Lifestyle) and the first to propose a lifestyle that was comprehensive (including all of the five critical areas of brain health and not just one).

Details of the Pilot Study

In 2008, we designed our first prospective pilot study to measure the effects of the brain health lifestyle on older independent-living residents of Farm Pond at Emeritus Assisted Living. Farm Pond was a wonderful setting to create a brain health campus and to conduct the study. It is a self-contained campus with three components to the continuum of care, including independent living, assisted living, and memory-impaired living. Our study focused on the independent-living residents. The other important positive quality about Farm Pond is that it had good leadership to make sure the study protocol was followed properly.

Our goal for conducting this study was to find answers to the following questions:

- Does the brain health lifestyle help to enhance memory in the form of verbal recall?
- Does the brain health lifestyle improve quality of life as reported by the actual residents?
- Does the brain health lifestyle improve quality of life as reported by an independent third party who worked at Farm Pond?
- Did the residents know more about their brain and brain health by the end of the study?

Sixteen volunteers were randomly selected from the independent-living residents to participate in the brain health lifestyle for six weeks. This group represented our experimental sample, and they would follow a relatively strict protocol for the entire six weeks of the study. An additional and separate ten residents from independent living made up the control sample. These persons were not part of the brain health lifestyle protocol, and they simply continued to live their lives as usual at Farm Pond during the six weeks of the study. The residents in the experiment group and the control sample were not significantly different on variables of age, education, marital status, or gender.

Each resident in both the control sample and experiment group underwent a baseline assessment that included measures of mental status, verbal recall with measures of immediate and delayed recall and recognition memory, mood, and basic knowledge of brain health. Each resident then underwent a post-study assessment using the same measures. The same person conducted the two assessments to provide some control on the actual assessment process, and different forms of the memory tool were used to minimize practice effects. I developed a self-report and third-party report that gauged quality of life and was completed by residents in the experimental sample only at the post-study period.

As expected from prospective studies, four residents from the experimental group and one resident from the control sample dropped out of the study prior to its conclusion. An analysis of the data indicated that the four who dropped out had lower mental status scores relative to those who remained in the study, suggesting that cognition may have been a variable predicting ability to sustain the six-week-long lifestyle. All residents were determined to be free of dementia, depression or other neuropsychiatric illness, substance abuse, uncontrolled hypertension or diabetes, and any uncorrected sensory deficit. The samples truly represented healthy, independent-living older adults.

Residents enrolled in the brain health lifestyle participated in one research-based activity within each of four domains of the lifestyle (physical activity, mental stimulation, spirituality, socialization), and they also consumed a special brain health diet. This occurred each day of the week for the entire six weeks. Examples of some of the activities within the physical activity domain included dance, walking, and aerobic exercise. Mental stimulation included sign language, Portuguese, discussion of the classics, and courses on the basics of the brain. Spirituality included prayer, meditation, and relaxation procedures. Socialization included field trips, recreational events, and games.

Results of the Pilot Study

People who enrolled in the brain health lifestyle program from the experimental group demonstrated no significant differences on measures of mental status, mood, or level of knowledge on the human brain at baseline relative to the control sample. However, changes in scores measured at post-study testing compared to baseline revealed trends to significance on measures of mental status and memory. Most striking, when the data from the experimental group was analyzed as a within-group measure, significant improvements were found on delayed recall and knowledge of the brain. That is, residents who participated in the six-week brain health lifestyle were able to recall presented information after a twenty-minute delay period better than they could prior to the start of the study. This is an important finding and may be the first to show a positive effect of a comprehensive lifestyle approach on enhanced memory.

Residents who participated in the brain health lifestyle demonstrated the expected significant improvement in self-reported knowledge of the human brain and how to keep their brain healthy. Quality of life was measured using a special tool developed by my questions dealing with a variety of aspects of one's life. Results indicate that the residents enrolled in the brain health lifestyle program reported positive sentiments about their life and mental and emotional functions after the study. They also expressed their belief that the brain health lifestyle was beneficial to them. They further expressed the belief that the brain health lifestyle is something that could be beneficial to everyone. Of equal interest were the results from the third-party ratings of quality of life. A designated person was asked to rate the resident's function, demeanor, social, and cognitive abilities at the conclusion of the lifestyle program. Similar to the self-report measures, the third-party ratings reflected improved overall function and quality of life for those who participated in the lifestyle program.

There was no change between samples or within the experimental sample on general mental status or mood. As no resident was found to be depressed upon entering the study, the finding of no improvement in depression is not unexpected. Regarding general mental status, the measure simply reflects basic information processing, and all residents who participated in this study performed near the ceiling at baseline and did not have room to improve by post-study.

Upon completion of the study, I met with the residents who participated in the six-week lifestyle. Results were discussed, and the residents provided important feedback about their experience. What we learned from the residents may have been more important than the positive data on memory and quality of life. Residents stated the lifestyle programming was "life changing" and reported, "It saved me, as I was not living since the death of my spouse," and "It brought me to life again and helped me get out of my room." These testimonials provide strong support for the power of the brain health lifestyle, and Farm Pond is now working to extend the program to all residents in independent living. Indeed, the original residents of the study agreed to be the ambassadors and lead the program on their campus.

This pilot is a small study of a few residents, and results need to be interpreted with caution. However, the finding of improved delayed recall and positive ratings on quality of life at the conclusion of the study are significant and deserving of attention. There is real reason to believe that a sustained and proactive brain health lifestyle that is comprehensive and integrated has potential to enhance cognitive functioning and quality of life in healthy older adults. There is also reason to believe that such a lifestyle should have similar effects in younger and middle-aged adults. With some modest alteration, the brain health lifestyle can also be followed by those who may require some assistance during the day, and even with those who have mild dementia. These are empirical questions that can be answered with more study and research. The pilot study is the first, albeit modest, empirical measure of the benefits one can obtain from following a brain health lifestyle, an early glimpse into the program's potential.

This study is a step that takes us beyond practical application of the brain health lifestyle to being able to cite empirical measures for its value. The next step is to replicate these early positive results with a larger and perhaps more diverse population. Ultimately, the brain health lifestyle should be a part of any prevention or wellness program, as the brain is the most important part of our being! Let's take a look at the five critical areas of brain health.

FIVE CRITICAL AREAS OF BRAIN HEALTH: AN OVERVIEW

The following provides a blueprint for the development of a brain health environment filled with the novel and complex.

The brain health lifestyle incorporates five distinct but integrated components: socialization, physical activity, mental stimulation, spirituality, and nutrition. Each of these components, or "slices to the brain health pie," encompasses research-based activities that have been documented to reduce the risk of dementia or to foster brain health. Together, these activities define the brain health lifestyle, which can be effectively applied in a culture committed to change.

Socialization

The first critical area to think about in order to promote a healthy brain lifestyle is the area of socialization. Research in both animals and humans indicates socialization is important to health and for reducing the risk of dementia. It is important, therefore, to remain integrated in the community, to build a growing network of family and friends, and to always have a role and purpose for getting up each day. Retirement, as a national policy, does not make sense for a nation that prioritizes brain health for its citizens. Retirement promotes isolation and passivity, which reduces the likelihood of building brain reserve and drives a brain toward disease. Socialization is so vital to brain health that it will be the first of the five areas of brain health we will explore at length in the following chapters. However, I do not want to convey that one domain is more important than the other.

Physical Activity

Physical activity relates to brain health because 25 percent of the blood, oxygen, and glucose from each heartbeat goes directly to the human brain. While the human brain weighs only two to four pounds on average, it demands more from each heartbeat than any other part of the body! It truly is the "central" nervous system. Knowing this simple fact, you can better appreciate why physical activity promotes brain health. The human brain consumes such a high level of glucose, oxygen, and blood because it cannot function without this energy source. Cells thrive from such blood flow and metabolize glucose for brain function, permitting rapid and efficient information processing. Even a brief period of slowed or no blood flow to a particular region of the brain can result in structural damage in the form of stroke, and this leads to loss of such functions as movement, language, and even personality change. You will learn much more about the crucial link between physical activity and brain health in Chapter 6.

Mental Stimulation

We have learned that novel and complex environments help to activate the cortex and conscious information processing that promotes development of brain reserve. Our ability to engage our brain daily in the novel and complex fosters mental stimulation and promotes brain health. This includes new learning, which actually involves a neurophysiological event or series of events that change our neural systems, our neural chemistry, and our brain function. This process can also assist with new brain cell development, or neurogenesis.

Animal studies have demonstrated neurogenesis in rodents exposed to enriched environments that include novel and complex stimuli. Human neurogenesis was demonstrated in a publication in 1998, with the neuroanatomical structure critical to learning, the hippocampus, representing the site of neurogenesis in both animals and humans. This supports the idea that the hippocampus and the role of learning are fundamental to our neural health and that our brains are agile and can adapt favorably in response to healthy stimuli. Environments that provide novel and complex stimuli are those most likely to be deemed "enriched," with the greatest likelihood of promoting brain reserve. Brain reserve refers to the development of increased cellular connections (synapses) that help to defend against or delay the onset of neurodegenerative diseases such as Alzheimer's.

A critical issue for everyone to remember is that the most sophisticated system for thinking, creating, problem solving, and basic academics is the human brain. It is critical for our society to turn inward for solving problems rather than relying only on gadgets or devices to do the work! Chapter 7 provides many specific ideas and suggestions for how you can enrich your own environment with the novel and complex.

Spirituality

We all lead very busy lifestyles, and surely, like many others, you feel the high stress of a fast-paced environment. It's no wonder we're doing so much damage to our own health because of it. This area, which I refer to as spirituality, addresses the need for all of us to slow down, to introspect, and to reduce stress in our lives. By engaging in a slower and more reflective life, we can impact our health and brains in a positive way.

Research indicates that animals exposed to environments that are too stimulating experience slowed brain development. Our own pace in life tends to be rapid and probably unhealthy. While most of us realize that we are going too fast and that we are involved in too many activities simultaneously, we have a hard time knowing how to slow down.

The brain demands stimulation, but it also can function best when it has rhythm and symmetry. Our hectic pace raises the probability of mental chaos, stress, and reduced cognitive efficiency. It also can lead to emotional breakdown. A brain health environment supports time for oneself, time to slow down, and time to keep the brain energized. I refer to this generally as spirituality. Of interest is the fact that an entire new field of study called *neurotheology* has emerged to study the relationship between spirituality, religion, and the brain. You will read more about neurotheology in Chapter 8 and also learn techniques for relaxation and stress abatement.

Nutrition

Food has the ability to alter thought processes, mood, and behavior. There is an entire new field of study called *nutritional neurosciences* that recognizes the impact of food on the function of the human brain. We also know that the human brain is 60 percent fat; indeed the brain is the fattest part of the body. It is believed that the lipid, or fatty, substance of the brain helps to insulate neural tracts, propelling information in a rapid and efficient manner. A brain that loses fat evinces slowed information processing, a maladaptive reality.

In recognition of this fact and our better understanding of the role of "free radicals" that originate as cellular breakdown with oxygen serving as a major catalyst, we can propose specific foods that supplement omega-3 fatty acids (good fat for the brain) and antioxidants that combat free radicals. In Chapter 9, a registered dietician discusses specific foods you can eat to get these healthy fats and other brain health foods.

ENGAGING WITH ALL OF THE CRITICAL AREAS OF BRAIN HEALTH

Your brain reacts favorably to enriched environments that promote the novel and complex, and that life provides us teachings about our brain every day. This includes growth of new brain cells and an increase in your brain reserve. Now that you've taken the time to review your current lifestyle and have taken the brain health inventory in the Introduction, you should be empowered by your newfound knowledge about yourself and your brain. Armed with an honest assessment of your current brain health lifestyle, you are ready to learn specific activities to promote brain health through the five critical areas of a healthy brain lifestyle.

As you read the following chapters, it is important that you think about why such activities promote brain health and whether you have these activities in your current lifestyle. Most important, think about what you will need to change in your current lifestyle to include these activities in your daily life. Now let's move ahead and take a more detailed look at each of the five areas that are critical to maximizing your brain health.

5

CRITICAL AREA 1: SOCIALIZATION

A social brain has a higher potential to be a healthy brain.

◉

Research teaches us that humans who isolate or segregate have a higher risk of dementia than those who remain integrated in society. A brain that does not receive social interaction becomes passive, and it is the complex and novel (and being with other people is likely to provide this) that is needed for development of brain reserve. When you engage in the novel and complex, you are stimulating your cortex, the conscious information-processing part of your brain, and you will promote the development of brain reserve. However, when you engage in behaviors that are passive and rote, you will use your subcortex, the part of the brain that helps you with procedures and subconscious action. This is not the pathway to development of brain reserve. This is a fascinating and robust finding that supports the importance of remaining involved and integrated in society and engaging in social interaction with others. It also underscores issues of personal meaning, role, and purpose and goes to the fundamental questions of why we are on the planet and what is our purpose.

The Health Risk of Retirement

Earlier on, I mentioned that dementia refers to loss of general intelligence, memory deficit, loss of other thinking abilities, personality change, and functional decline. Socialization is key to ward off precipitant mental aging. There are nearly one hundred causes of dementia, and Alzheimer's is the leading cause in the United States. Socialization's link to brain health might be explained by the opportunity for communication, critical thought, creativity, and emotional expression, including intimacy, chemical connection, touch, expression of role and purpose, and recreation that arises when two or more humans interact. Personal meaning and identity might also be a result of interpersonal activity or the dedication to an entity or mission "larger than oneself." When we interact with others on a consistent basis, we create opportunities to learn from them. Kofi Annan, former secretary general of the United Nations, said that the elders in his village were considered "libraries," and that when an older person died, the village lost a library. If we think of others as libraries filled with information, it makes sense to interact with as many people as we can to better ourselves. Additionally, if you maintain an active social network, your own personal development can be enhanced, and the ability to create your own identity and personal mission on Earth can be formed. This process can be enhanced by those in your social network providing you feedback, listening to you, and helping to shape the person you become.

HEALTHY BRAIN TIP

Stay involved in your community at every age, do not retire, and have a personally meaningful reason for getting up each day!

I had the unique opportunity to provide a brief presentation on brain health in America at the National Press Club a couple of years ago (see asaging.org for the report of this expert panel on brain health in America). I voiced my opposition to our national policy of retirement, since it contradicts nearly everything I know about brain health. A nation enlightened on brain health encourages active involvement across the life span and does not reinforce or encourage removal of oneself from society to a passive and potentially isolated environment when an individual has reached a certain age. As I travel the nation teaching audiences about the brain, I always underscore the importance of remaining involved in meaningful ways—such as being engaged by your community and social surroundings. I discourage retirement, as some identify their worth and very being by their occupation! There is a type of psychological retirement that gets missed with so many who literally count the days and hours down to their "retirement." More planning is needed to prepare for your time and purpose once the particular job is gone. Unfortunately, some of us will be confronted with unexpected loss prior to our declared retirement date, and we have not prepared psychologically for this. Surveys of baby boomers (76 million Americans born between 1946 and 1964) indicate retirement is being redefined and boomers will change their career many times and will likely continue to work later into life relative to their parents.

As retirement can propel one into a state of isolation and segregation where he or she is no longer a vital component of society, the brain will react by becoming passive. Even if you do not have formal employment, your brain will continue to need novel and complex stimulation, and a conscious effort to define and redefine your personal mission in life will help you to have purpose and a reason for getting up and out into the world every day.

Depending on where you live, there may be mandatory retirement (based on an incredibly invalid construct of chronological age) for some occupations, but I believe the development of hobbies beginning in early to middle life (twenties to sixties) is important. A hobby provides challenges for the brain. Multiple hobbies reflect a robust brain with neural networks that have been nurtured. Development of hobbies is a highly important behavior and a challenge for the baby boomers. Hobby development creates an enriched environment and provides a vehicle for the brain to experience the novel and complex.

Hobbies also provide a wonderful vehicle for socialization, and indeed, it might be the social network you have developed that fosters your hobby. Hobbies, like talents, can be shared with others, and others can benefit from your hobbies. What hobbies do you have, and do you have interests that you have been resisting or putting off for some time? Take one such interest and get started today. You are on your way to building brain reserve!

Promote Brain Health Through Socialization

Every community has a variety of clubs, organizations, and formal groups that seek membership. These may be part of a local church, school, or neighborhood. While most of these memberships require volunteer time, they provide the value of socialization and contribution to an ongoing enterprise. What will it take for you to explore the opportunities in your community where you can provide input and value? What skills do you have to offer? We tend to be too busy to think about such questions or to explore such issues. These are interesting questions that require some deep thought and time. If you have discovered your true mission, the opportunity exists to align what it is you are called to do with what you actually do. Happiness and productivity are typically the outcome of such alignment.

By first understanding your own inner talents and passions, you will be able to define what you are "called to do." This, in turn, will lead to your sharing your passion with others to benefit the community around you. Social networks and socialization can be a wonderful outcome for one person identifying an inner talent and sharing it in a passionate way with others around him or her.

You have a wonderful list of talents that probably have not been tapped. Take a few moments and prepare a list of talents you think you possess. It does not matter if you have expressed them yet. These talents are most likely not related to your occupation or job description, and they probably represent those things that you would like to pursue "if I only had the time." Once you have made your list of talents or skills, begin to relate them to the list of organizations or clubs in your community—this will allow you to engage with your community and a network of people who have similar interests and passions.

HEALTHY BRAIN TIP
Develop hobbies, identify your own innate talents, and align them with ongoing involvement in groups or organizations in your community.

Overcome Isolation to Connect with People

A difficult reality for many people is the feeling of isolation. Whether this is something you experience now or experience when older, it's important to combat in order to promote brain health. Isolation represents a risk factor for dementia, and a recent study found that "loneliness" also relates to an increased risk of dementia. A lonely brain is a brain that is emotionally isolated and perhaps depressed.

Overcoming isolation is not only an important initiative for you but also for those around you. Perhaps you have an older parent who is functional but is not exposed to opportunities for socialization. It is important for families or the caregiver to rally and make assertive attempts to get their mother or father out of the house or room and to help her or him recapture a connection with ongoing life. This can require strong suggestions and recommendations to encourage parents to engage in social functions; this may even involve you literally taking them to events. While your parent may not like your motives initially, you can continue to explain the issue of brain health and risk of dementia to your parent. There is no greater motivator to behavior change than loss of independence, particularly for the older adult.

In order to maintain or maximize the chance for independence, we need to remain active, not passive, and we need to remain integrated in society. Socialization is critical. Do you notice any potential alignments where your talents can increase the value of a particular organization or club? You might even have the entrepreneurial spirit to begin your own club, group, or business using your talents to lead the way! The point of this exercise is to realize that socialization is important to brain health, that identifying opportunities for socialization in your community and combining that with your own innate talents can foster an enriched environment for your brain health. Let's take a look at a couple of ways to improve upon socialization in all areas of your life.

Socialization at Home

Families represent a natural social group, but sometimes family members get scattered, and it can be difficult to have family time. It is important to prioritize family time so everyone can be together. There does not need to be a formal program or event. Families can simply sit and chat, watch a movie, take a walk, or play a game. Friends and relatives can join the family to maintain an active and growing social network. Remaining integrated and involved and not feeling lonely are health-promoting, especially for the brain. Consider these tips to improve socialization at home:

- Establish a family night or two during the week when all or at least several family members will unite as a group.
- Have fun together and play games, recreate, take walks, or simply talk.
- Have one family meal a day with no television, so that you can share stories, concerns, and goals.
- Try something new together, such as a museum, zoo, or library visit—these are great ways to promote socialization.
- Invite friends and family members to your home.
- Promote family nights and explore events like outdoor symphonies, ballet, theater, movies, documentaries, or lectures.

The home represents many things to each individual on a very personal level. One thing the home probably has not been considered is a setting for brain health. However, this can change, and with some small adjustments, the home can become an enriched environment healthy for the brain.

Socialization in the Workplace

It may seem easy to promote socialization in a corporate setting because there are so many people. However, the corporate setting does not easily facilitate in-depth interaction, and most person-to-person contacts may be superficial or task-based. A corporate setting interested in promoting brain health should encourage opportunities for group interaction, both business and recreational. Meeting and interacting with new people provide the novel and complex environment important to brain health. It's important that you get out of your comfort zone and work to promote a more enriched social environment. You can learn much and offer much when you work in an unfamiliar part of the company with different people. Here are some ways that you can promote socialization at work:

- Create group functions and problem-solving opportunities at work.
- Encourage interdisciplinary functions and idea sharing.
- Engage in workplace functions, like happy hour or an office party. This may include dance, food, and learning opportunities all at once.

- Encourage recreational or entertainment functions outside the work setting.
- Encourage fun and friendly team competition in the work setting, like team-building games.
- Create a list of community organizations that the employees can review and decide to get involved with.

By integrating the activities within the five critical domains of my brain health lifestyle into the work site, you can begin the process of turning your office setting into a brain health center.

Promote Socialization in Other Areas of Your Life

There are other ways you can promote socialization within your community. It is also probably fair to say that most of the social activities performed take place outside of work and home. It's important to explore these other opportunities. Remember, research indicates socialization reduces the risk of dementia, particularly for older persons. It is important to recognize what opportunities exist in your community for socialization and what forums exist that offer a potential for providing a wonderful setting for group activities within your community or to participate in other activities. Such opportunities can also create new friendships and help offset potential loneliness and even mood disorders. Consider the following ideas for how you can engage your community and surroundings to increase socialization:

- Coordinate ongoing social gatherings for dialogue and debate on a particular issue of the day.
- Find out if there are any book clubs or discussion groups you can join.
- Engage in forums available to you and your local community in the areas of art, music, dance, poetry, and storytelling.
- Consider starting your own social network in your community that can facilitate ongoing personal interaction, sharing of ideas, and creativity. You can create your own formal dance or wine-tasting events.
- Seek out lecture series with local and national speakers; this is a great way to explore new environments and social situations.
- Develop relationships with local restaurants, bowling alleys, country clubs, theatres, and museums that can promote social functions that you can attend.
- Think about your community goals. Explore local community groups and organizations and seek involvement. This could include promoting awareness for your passion and interests, like getting involved with a local charity or social concerns committee.
- Use modern technology to increase socialization. The computer and the Internet represent wonderful tools to bring more people from all across the planet into a social network. Facebook, MySpace, and Twitter are examples

of websites that encourage socialization. Intergenerational activity is enhanced with the computer, as grandparents can communicate and interact with their grandchildren on a daily basis. There is a wonderful new social networking business called MyWayVillage (www.mywayvillage .com) that provides computers and training to older adults to remain connected to their families. This is another excellent example of using new technologies to keep older adults and all of us socially integrated.

TIPS TO PROMOTE BRAIN HEALTH: QUICK REVIEW

- Identify what your reason for being alive is and then follow it. You will most likely take this inner passion and talent and share it with others around you, which will create the social network that is vital for brain health promotion.
- Work on building new relationships and reinforce existing ones. This includes one-to-one interpersonal interaction, group work, and use of the computer for social networking.
- Work to resolve existing conflicts with others. By resolving conflicts with another person or group of people, we create the opportunity to work with them rather than against them. Recall that every person is a library of information, and we need to be able to access their stories through open dialogue. Removing tensions and conflict will help to make this a reality.
- Develop hobbies to build new interests and build brain reserve. Identify what interests and talents you have. Select one or two that you are passionate about and begin the process of identifying clubs or

groups in your community with similar passion. Once again, your hobbies can be shared with others and may represent the vehicle to create a new social network.

- Remain active in pursuits that are meaningful to you. By understanding your passions, you can develop your personal mission that gives you meaning and purpose. This leads to a natural sharing with others and social networking.

6

CRITICAL AREA 2: PHYSICAL ACTIVITY

It is the physically active, not the passive, brain that will benefit most.

◉

It is an amazing fact that your brain demands 25 percent of the blood from each heartbeat! I often refer to this as "market share"—and real narcissism—on the part of your brain. There is a real reason we call the brain the central nervous system, as it really is the center of the universe. It's easy to understand why physical activity is so important to brain health when you recognize how much benefit the brain derives from each heartbeat. We need to have a healthy heart that pumps blood efficiently for healthy brain function, and physical activity such as exercise has been proven to be a robust correlate to heart health. Today we are able to say with confidence that many different forms of physical activity are also good for your brain, so we need to get moving. When you are moving, you can feel good about the fact that you are making your brain very happy!

Animals that ran on a wheel generated new brain cells in studies conducted in the late 1950s. This research underscores the importance of physical activity to animal brain health. The same relationship between physical activity and brain health appears to be true for humans. It is important to understand *why* physical activity relates to brain health. Every time your heart beats, 25 percent of the blood and nutrients from that one heartbeat goes directly to your brain. We have known for some time that physical exercise is critical to cardiac health, but research is now beginning to support a similar value for physical exercise to brain health!

EXERCISE AND THE HUMAN BRAIN

A 2006 study published in the *Journal of Gerontology* found that as little as three hours a week of brisk walking, an excellent aerobic exercise, increases blood flow to the brain and may trigger neurochemical changes that increase production of new brain cells. The regions of the brain most affected by the aerobic exercise included the frontal lobes, important for complex thinking, reasoning, and attention, and the corpus callosum, the bundle of white matter that bridges the two sides of the brain. This brain study is important for several reasons:

- The results further support brain plasticity and new brain cell development in humans.
- The study was conducted on persons aged sixty to seventy-nine, indicating brain health can improve in later life. This

is consistent with animal brain research showing positive effects at advanced ages. Remember, I do not believe in a critical period of brain development unless it is defined as life! The traditional idea of a "critical period of brain development" being in the first five or six years of your life is no longer considered valid. With our new understanding of the human brain and neural plasticity, we recognize the brain can be shaped for health across the entire life span. In this regard, the critical period of brain development is probably best characterized as life itself, from the time we are developing in our mother's womb until our last day.

- This may be the first study to demonstrate healthy structural changes in the human brain with physical activity, a finding we know exists for animals.
- We know a relationship exists between physical changes in the brain, positive and negative, and functional or cognitive ability.

Many other studies have shown that physical activity and exercise such as walking promote the health of the human brain. Research has demonstrated an increased relationship between development of the myelin sheath, the lipid substance that surrounds brain cells and nerve tracts propelling rapid information flow, and exercise; increased learning and exercise; increased test scores in school and exercise; and even improvement in mood and physical exercise. Mobility and blood flow are critical for human beings and necessary for brain health. This relationship likely exists at all ages and with healthy and diseased brains. Other research suggests that walking on a daily basis or at least several times a week can reduce the risk of dementia.

This finding again supports the relationship between physical activity and the reduced risk of brain disease.

Interestingly, there appears to be a dosing effect; the more you walk during the week, the more positive effect it has for the brain. People know they should be walking daily, and they can even specify the need to walk about ten thousand steps daily, but unfortunately, being educated about what's good for you does not necessarily translate into action or behavior. I read recently that only about 35 percent of this country's population is involved in a formal and consistent exercise program! I can tell you to walk on a daily basis and to try and take ten thousand steps daily. However, what are the chances of you actually doing it? It takes a little motivation and a few tools to get you started. I recommend that you purchase a pedometer at any local shopping mall or sports store. You will derive tremendous value for your purchase, as the pedometer will keep track of your daily steps, and it will also remind you to walk. I always recommend you buy one for a loved one in your family; it makes a great birthday present. Have some fun with it!

BRAIN HEALTH TIP

Get physically active with at least three hours of aerobic exercise a week, and walk for distance three to five times per week. It is recommended that we all walk around ten thousand steps daily! Purchase a pedometer to keep count.

PROMOTE BRAIN HEALTH THROUGH PHYSICAL ACTIVITY

You now know that aerobic exercise, particularly walking, on a daily basis has a clear functional benefit to your brain. Physical activity helps to increase brain health, and you have been taught a practical tip, purchasing a pedometer, to help change your behavior. You will be interested to find out that there are other physical activities you can enjoy that relate to reduced risk of dementia. The interesting thing about these brain-boosting activities is that you will need to use both sides of your body. I am often surprised by the fact that most of us not only have a dominant side, but that we have almost completely neglected our non-dominant side. It is important to understand that each side of your body is controlled by the opposite side of the brain. As such, most of us have essentially ignored one half of our brain, so begin to champion both sides of the brain.

An Ambidextrous Brain Is a Healthier Brain

Building an ambidextrous brain involves some basic and practical steps. First, it is important to understand that your arms and legs represent two of the major pathways into the brain. The left side of our body is controlled by the right hemisphere of our brain, while the right side of our body is controlled by our left hemisphere of our brain. Most of us have a dominant hand

and leg. We tend to use these limbs much more often than our non-dominant limbs, and this is why our non-dominant limbs are weaker and less coordinated. Underlying the fact that these limbs are weaker and less coordinated than our dominant limbs is the fact that we do not have sufficient neural circuitry in our brains to help these limbs function as well as our dominant limbs. There is only one way to change that, and it is to use our non-dominant limbs more often. Writing with your non-dominant hand on a daily basis, dribbling a basketball with your non-dominant hand, building puzzles and putting things together with your non-dominant hand, and even kicking and jumping with your non-dominant leg are examples of exercises you can do to build up the neural circuitry in different parts of your non-dominant hemisphere.

The reason an ambidextrous brain is so important to health is that if we fall victim to a stroke or structural damage in one hemisphere, we will be better able to adjust to the loss if we have sufficient development of other areas of the brain to compensate for and even pick up the functional responsibility of the damaged region.

Other physical activities known to promote brain heath include dance, particularly the tango and other pattern dances, as it has been shown to reduce the risk of dementia. I am not sure we have the ability to specify how much dance or how often we should dance yet, but this behavior appears to be healthy for the brain. Gardening and knitting are two activities that also relate to reduced risk of dementia. Notice that dance, gardening, and knitting demand use of both sides of the body. In thinking about how knitting and gardening might lead to brain health, it is useful to consider what the brain is asked to do with these activities. For example, with gardening your brain will be asked to plan into the future and engage in visuospatial function and visuomotor skill. This says nothing about the stress reduction gardening might offer. We need to learn that a health effect can be derived by things other than pills, liquids, and shots!

BRAIN HEALTH TIP

Specific physical activities that promote brain health include the following:

- Walking about ten thousand steps daily or thirty minutes a day
- Gardening
- Aerobic exercise three times a week
- Knitting
- Dancing

Physical Activity at Home

The great thing about the home setting for brain health is that each of the activities can be family-based. Children will most likely model what you, the parents, do, and getting the children's brains involved in a brain health lifestyle early can translate into a more positive benefit. Here are some ways you can be more active to promote your brain health at home:

- Take nightly or daily walks with the entire family. Each family member can own a pedometer and keep track of his or her steps on a daily basis. Remember, ten thousand steps a day is a good goal for most. It is also important to try and walk or engage in movement of some type for thirty minutes a day. This need not occur in thirty consecutive minutes; cumulative time throughout the day is fine.
- Consider a dance class or two for the family. Pattern dance is always a good one to try and can include the waltz, polka, and tango.
- Invest in simple exercise equipment to have in your home, like a treadmill, bike, or step-master. If you don't have the space, you can easily set out time to go jogging or running! Encourage your family to do this with you. The important thing is to perform such aerobic exercise several times a week to increase the cardiovascular output. Remember, your brain demands 25 percent of the blood from each heartbeat.

We all need to be active and mobile. Walking, jogging, swimming, biking, aerobics, dancing, and even gardening and knitting are wonderful activities for brain health promotion. You can feel good about the fact that such physical activity will produce increased blood flow to the brain and help the brain to function more efficiently, enhance mood, increase cognitive ability, and even boost energy levels. So get up and get moving!

Physical Activity in the Workplace

It's no wonder it's hard to find time to be physically active—since most of our time may be spent at work—but some workplaces offer another environment where you can be physically active.

One example is the growing number of businesses and companies that promote wellness programs, including providing space at the work site to exercise and engage in physical activity. Some companies even provide incentives to their employees to exercise in the hope of generating a more productive workforce, a healthier workforce, and a lowered utilization of health care services. Here are some practical tips you can follow to increase your physical activity at work:

- Inquire if your company has a wellness program, and ask how to enroll.
- Join the walking club at your work setting, and utilize the gym or exercise facility that the company has or provides membership to as a benefit.
- Make a conscious attempt to walk at lunch, use the steps instead of the elevator or escalator, and try parking far from the front door and then walk briskly to the entrance.
- Purchase a pedometer and wear it to work. As you know, the pedometer will provide you immediate feedback on the number of steps you take daily. In addition, your coworkers will also see your pedometer, and you might be able to get the entire staff to purchase pedometers. I have worked with large companies that actually have contests between

departments on number of steps taken during a particular month. Results can be posted, and small rewards can be presented to those who walk the most. It can be fun!

- Physical activity can be one way to develop team-building exercises, which might include developing team goals that are reached using physical activity. This could be fun and will also increase socialization as well.

- Ask if your place of employment has an outdoor space for physical activity. This may include a walking trail, exercise stations, outdoor exercise equipment, bikes, or areas for gardening. You and your peers can enjoy the benefits of getting outside and engaging in physical exercise. This can become very important to the employees once they learn about the relationship between gardening and reduction in the risk of dementia.

- Ask if your company has a relationship with a dance club where you can register for dance lessons. You might even speak to human resources about including dance lessons at the place of work as part of the wellness program. Dance has been shown to promote brain health.

Promoting Physical Activities in Other Areas of Your Life

There is no doubt that movement, exercise, and daily physical activity are good for your general health and indeed for your brain health. I have provided you some practical tips on how to engage in physical activity at home and in the work setting. It is important to note that we all have other environments in our lives where we can engage in physical activity. To understand the importance of daily physical activity, you are reminded that there are enough studies now that indicate the following relationship between physical activity and brain health:

- Aerobic exercise three times a week reduces the risk of Alzheimer's.
- Students who exercise regularly enjoy better test scores.
- Walking and dancing on a daily basis reduces the risk of dementia.
- Wearing a pedometer, a small device that clips on your belt and measures the number of steps you take daily, relates to better health.
- Regular physical exercise is related to reduction in the severity of depressive symptoms.

These studies provide sufficient support to the idea and recommendation that daily physical activity is critical to your general and your brain health. As discussed earlier, physical activity is directly related to cardiovascular function, and the human brain demands 25 percent of the blood from each heartbeat. This physiological fact is the underlying explanation as to why physical activity promotes brain health in the form of cognitive and emotional well-being.

The question becomes, how do you incorporate physical activity into your daily life outside of work and even when away from home? Here are some other ideas:

- If you are in a large building or a mall, use the steps and not the elevator or escalator.
- If you are an individual who travels for a living, make sure to use hotels that have a pool so you can swim and a fitness room to get your daily workout in.
- Consider joining a recreational league for any of your favorite sports; you can even consider coaching a youth sport and use the time to exercise with the players.
- If possible, use a bike to travel to local events rather than your car.

BRAIN HEALTH TIP

For those who may have physical limitations and are unable to exert themselves much, you can still get moving through slow, resistance exercise like stationary biking or even low-impact activities like those offered by virtual reality video-game systems like Nintendo's Wii Sports and Wii Fit.

The important idea in this section is that physical activity is critical to brain health and that we can apply different forms of physical activity to the settings we visit in our lives—our schools, libraries, and places of work—where we may spend many hours. It is important to think how you can apply the physical-activity part of the brain health lifestyle wherever you are and help to create brain-healthy environments by example. Remember, it does not matter where you are, your brain will always demand 25 percent of the blood from each heartbeat.

Physical activity will not only help to promote the blood flow from the heart, but such vigorous movement will ultimately help your brain be as healthy as possible.

TIPS TO PROMOTE BRAIN HEALTH: QUICK REVIEW

- Regular physical exercise correlates with enhanced learning, improved cognition, reduced risk of Alzheimer's, and lessening of depressive symptoms. Your brain demands 25 percent of the blood from each heartbeat.
- Research supports a relationship between walking, aerobic exercise, dance, knitting, and gardening and reduction in the risk of dementia. Allot time in each day for physical activity.
- No matter where you drive, you can always park a good distance from the front entrance. This will force you to walk and help you to get some of those ten thousand steps that are a daily goal.
- Enroll in classes like yoga, tai chi, or a dance course.
- Invest in a pedometer. Remember, it only takes about ten thousand steps a day to get you closer to a healthier brain!

7

Critical Area 3: Mental Stimulation

How brilliant is a system that can create something
that was not there a second before?

◉

Perhaps the most obvious lifestyle factor affecting brain health is mental stimulation. The human brain seeks stimulation regardless of age, and this stimulation likely begins in the womb. As we've learned, the brain gets stimuli from enriched environments, which helps to facilitate development of *brain reserve*, the term used to describe the brain's development of dendrites and brain cell interaction. Brain reserve helps your brain to delay the onset of neurodegenerative diseases, such as dementia and Alzheimer's, so the more you have, the more likely your mind is to stay young and sharp. Ultimately, environmental input can shape the structure and function of your brain across your entire life span, which is why it's important to create environments for yourself that optimize the development of brain reserve.

Mental stimulation is critical to the development and health of the human brain. Cognitive stimulation of the brain begins in the womb and continues to have tremendous health-promoting value until you die. How does an enriched environment promote mental stimulation through novel and complex stimuli? Creativity and innovation are two critical thought processes to promote in any setting dedicated to brain health. Albert Einstein often asserted that a less structured environment best unleashes the imagination and creativity of the brain. Unfortunately, our traditional environments, such as school and work, tend to adhere to a highly structured and programmatic approach to life. We need to be able to think more creatively and approach the same problems of life with increased imagination.

The human brain can be stimulated using many different types of information and stimuli, though novelty and complexity remain necessary ingredients for any stimulus to be considered to promote brain health. Novelty and complexity are so important because such stimuli are processed by the cortex, where brain reserve is best generated. We do not want to engage in activities any more than is necessary that are rote and passive, that probably are most related to the subcortex, and that most likely do not contribute much to development of brain reserve. We all have to do rote activities like putting on clothes and brushing our teeth. True mental stimulation can only be gained through such activities as reading; writing; traveling; engaging in creative pursuits, such as art and music; game-playing; learning new languages, including sign language; developing hobbies; and participating in a critical exchange of thoughts, like debating.

Research Reveals the Benefits of Active Mental Stimulation

Research on the human brain and brain health is helping all of us understand more about our brains and how to apply specific activities in our daily lives to promote our own brain health.

Language and Brain Development

Research shows that language appears to be critical when it comes to brain development. The sophistication of the language system in young adulthood might actually be predictive of brain health in late life. Dr. D. A. Snowdon, an epidemiologist who has spent many years following a cohort of nuns with an interest in the relationship between their lifestyle and health (known as the "nun study"), including brain health, has found that the number of ideas expressed in diaries written by twenty-one-year-old females predicted percentage of tangles in the brain, a marker of Alzheimer's, nearly sixty years later.

Dr. Snowdon proposed that language sophistication in early life might mark a well-developed brain, resistant to neurodegenerative changes later in life. In contrast, a language system not well developed in early life may mark a vulnerable brain, at risk for neurodegenerative changes in later life. This suggests that we can all work to develop our writing and speaking abilities early in life as one means of building a healthier brain and perhaps a resistance to neurodegenerative disease later in life. This is a good example of how mental stimulation early in life can have long-lasting positive effects on brain health.

There is also some interesting work done researching brain development by teaching infants sign language prior to their neurological ability to speak. Infants can learn about twenty signs prior to being able to speak words. When the infants exposed to sign language are followed, they have greater articulation abilities, and their IQ is higher by the second grade relative to controls (children not taught sign language). As we learned earlier, higher IQ early in life relates to reduced risk of dementia later in life. Once again, interventions early in life that enhance IQ and develop the language system appear to be examples of proactive brain health. These studies underscore the critical point that brain health is a lifelong pursuit and that risk of dementia and Alzheimer's may actually begin in childhood, but it's never too late to promote brain health by learning a new language, even sign language!

Each of these studies supports the beneficial effects that mental stimulation has on brain health, with that benefit lasting many years. They also help people understand what types of activities are not only mentally stimulating but what specific activities promote brain health.

Developing Cognitive Skills Through Mental Stimulation

Because your brain is the single greatest information-processing system in the universe, it is not surprising that many people focus on mental stimulation as perhaps the only factor for brain health. It is important to remember that the human brain is not just a cognitive processor; it is an emotional, motor, and creative system in addition. Mental stimulation can help not only with the development of cognitive skills, but also with processing of emotion and even learning of methods to enhance motor and coordination skills.

Studies have indicated, for example, that higher levels of education not only lead to reduced risk of Alzheimer's disease but can also help to reduce the risk of depression. Our ability to cope with difficulty in our lives is enhanced as we learn more. At this point we do not have one index or metric for mental stimulation other than the intelligence quotient (IQ), though a company called Fit Brains, online at fitbrains.com, is working on a Fit Brains Index (FBI), and you can also derive your own brain health lifestyle score by completing the survey in the Introduction of this book. Both of these are meant to provide you with gross measures of strengths and weaknesses in your cognitive FBI and brain health lifestyle and are not scientifically based.

Appealing to the cognitive focus of the human brain, there are numerous computer-based products being sold to the consumer that aim to provide memory and other mental exercises. You can challenge yourself with these mental exercises on a daily basis with the hope of improving your different cognitive or thinking abilities. Use the software on your own computer or visit an Internet site where you can complete your mental workout. A 2006 study by Dr. Sherry Willis and her colleagues at Penn State University is one of the first to document long-term positive effects of cognitive training on everyday function in older adults. We will likely continue to see new businesses emerging around the desire for improving the mental aspects of the brain. This represents another example of a cultural shift toward brain health!

IMPORTANCE OF LIFELONG LEARNING

Learning new and difficult information provides a short-term benefit that includes enhanced intelligence. Perhaps more important, however, a long-term benefit is also derived, in which the brain builds brain reserve that can help to delay onset of neurodegenerative diseases such as Alzheimer's disease. The very function of learning today, therefore, is health promoting, with the greatest positive effect taking place many years later! This is the precise reason I believe learning should be part of our health care plan and encouraged by the major health care payer systems such as Medicare and others. A nation enlightened to brain health for its citizens will promote behaviors that encourage learning across the life span. If you engage in consistent learning and activities that promote mental stimulation beginning in early life, your risk of developing dementia will decrease. This will result in a general reduction in costs for treating dementia later in life.

Learning is a critical function to the existence, survival, and development of humans. Our brains are literally changed from one second to the next when we learn something new. The hippocampus takes the information our brains collect via the sensory pathways and helps the brain to transition that information from a short-term buffer to a longer-term storage in a specific region of our cortex. I view learning as a health-promoting behavior because it most likely helps the brain develop new brain cells, increases brain reserve, alters our neurochemistry in a way that may help alleviate mood disorder, and may ultimately be critical in the brain's ability to fight off dementia later in life. It is a short step to take from viewing learning as a behavior that promotes brain health to begin to encourage everyone to actually engage in lifelong learning.

I have had the pleasure of learning about the value and fun of Elderhostel and Osher lifelong learning programs. Hundreds of thousands of older adults are enrolling in university classroom work as part of their "retirement." What used to be the beach or the golf course is now a book and classroom! Indeed, research indicates education is a major factor contributing to longevity and health. The actual event of learning something new involves the laying down of a new neural network that was not there before. It bears repeating that with continued learning, the brain develops a rich network of neural associations we refer to as brain reserve. It is this brain reserve that helps to delay onset of neurodegenerative disorders such as Alzheimer's.

We need to invest in learning prior to onset of dementia and indeed to combat dementia, as we are expending millions of dollars in dementia care on an annual basis, and this is only going to become a bigger problem worldwide. In order to be proactive, we need to begin very early in life. Our children will more likely care for their brains if they understand this wonderful part of their being. The earlier the education occurs, the earlier a proactive lifestyle for brain health can be started. As we learned earlier, the types of environments we expose our brains to early in life relate to the health of our brains later in life.

BRAIN HEALTH TIP

Develop your language system, learn a new language, read and write daily, and expose your brain to sign language! Sign on to fitbrains.com and get started on learning more about your brain and begin your daily brain-fitness program.

PROMOTE BRAIN HEALTH THROUGH MENTAL STIMULATION

Mental stimulation that is active, difficult, and new will foster development of neural connections in the cortex, the primary site of brain-reserve development. Mental stimulation can be engaged by many things, from reading, to writing, to brain puzzles, to problem-solving games, and of course, some activities such as language development that have a universal human benefit for brain health—important at all ages across the entire life span.

Stimulate Your Brain with Games, Reading and Writing, Music, and Travel

We can recognize what we already do that might be healthy and also identify resources in our environment to include in our brain health lifestyle. A good example is research that supports a relationship between game playing and brain health. Most of us have enjoyed playing board games with family or friends even though we never considered it a brain-healthy exercise. The same can be said for some of the older (solitaire) and newer individual games (sudoku) and the computerized brain health fitness programs such as Fitbrains.com. Once again, these mentally stimulating activities provide the brain with novel and complex input that can help build brain reserve and brain health.

Games. Traditional board games have also been studied, and a publication several years ago in a major medical journal reported a relationship between playing board games and reduction in the risk of dementia. My interpretation of this finding is that playing board games can and should be included in a brain health lifestyle. I was asked by a major well-known company to promote board-game playing on a national media tour. This was both fun and important, and the research on brain health made this a consumer-friendly and necessary communication. Recall that stimuli that are novel and complex are most likely to stimulate the cortex, where brain reserve is developed, and it is the novel and complex that lead to buildup of brain reserve.

You probably never thought of your family game of Scrabble or Monopoly as a brain health workout. Other games such as poker, bridge, sudoku, and crossword puzzles have brain-health-promoting effects so long as they are "novel and complex." Once any activity becomes "rote and passive," the positive brain health effects have been reduced, so remember to increase the level of difficulty when you engage in these activities. At the neurophysiological level, you want to maintain stimulation of the cortex by doing things that are novel, complex, and challenging.

Reading and Writing. Another way to stimulate your mind is to read and write on a daily basis, which is great brain exercise. By engaging the hippocampus, the part of the brain that is responsible for new learning and memory, we most likely foster new brain-cell development and increase brain reserve. The more you stimulate and massage your hippocampus, the more learning occurs, and the better chance for an increased IQ. In fact, writing sentences as a teenager or young adult that include numerous ideas has been shown to promote brain health even sixty to seventy years later. Also, writing with passion rather than a more stoic statement of fact has been correlated with increased longevity. Perhaps passion is an important component of living a long and healthy life. Try to read new material on new topics and write with the intent of expressing ideas. Remember, try to write with your non-dominant hand a few minutes a day to build an ambidextrous brain!

Brain Health Tip

Enroll in a lifelong learning program in your community or at your local university. Encourage your local school board to integrate curricula on the basics of the human brain within the elementary school—be proactive!

Music. Classical music has been found to have a relationship to learning in children. It is not uncommon to observe classical music being played in some classrooms during study period or perhaps even during a test. Study time at home can be enhanced with background music, especially classical. Some research suggests classical music played for the baby developing in the womb may have neurological benefit, so there's definitely promise here for you to reap brain health benefits from this practice! I also encourage you to try and learn to play a musical instrument. It is true that learning to play a musical instrument is harder as you age, but your brain can learn an instrument at any age. Do not be afraid to develop that dormant part of your brain!

BRAIN HEALTH TIP
Start to play those wonderful board games again, learn a musical instrument, and tune in to a classical radio station.

Travel. Travel has been shown to reduce the risk of dementia or, better said, to increase brain health. Consider how this
behavior might promote brain health. You already know that
the best environment for your brain is to surround yourself
with the complex and novel. The whole point of traveling away
from home is to leave your familiar surrounding and expose
your brain to a novel and complex environment. As a result,
you will use your cortex to navigate, and you will probably find
it exciting and maybe frustrating at times. Interestingly, as you
stay in that new environment, you will become more familiar
and comfortable. The novel and complex will become rote and
passive with time. Every day you travel to and from work and
home and essentially do not use your cortex. Your subcortex
has the mental maps of your home and neighborhood encoded,
and the processing tends to be rote or subconscious. New environments are more stimulating for your brain. The other nice
thing about travel is that you will meet new people who contribute to your enriched environment!

BRAIN HEALTH TIP
Try and take a trip or two this year to a new surrounding and enjoy the
brain health benefits!

Mental Stimulation at Home

How can your home become an enriched environment, and what things can you do in your home to promote mental stimulation and the entire five components of the brain health lifestyle? The home can be a great place for mental stimulation. Unfortunately we tend to rely on televisions, computers, iPods, and our cell phones for entertainment. These technologies require passive processing that does not stimulate the cortex, which is not the right way to stimulate the mind. Remember that in order for activities to be stimulating, they must be novel and complex in order to maximize development of brain reserve and brain health. It is important to understand that we can use these relatively new technologies to promote brain health. Indeed, research indicates that reading new information on the Internet stimulates the brain and that listening to music on the iPod can stimulate memory in those who suffer from dementia. It is true that these technologies can provide stimulating learning opportunities, but we need to be vigilant about our brain's need to be active and not passive most of the time. Once again, the nice thing about the home setting from a brain health perspective is that the lifestyle can be applied as a family. Here are some ideas for how you can increase mental (cortical) stimulation at home:

- Participate in activities that are creative and artistic. Set out a structured time during the day for creative writing and have each family member share their creation.
- Establish a weekly night for board games and get the entire family involved. Playing board games has been related to a

reduction in the risk of dementia. Crossword puzzles and sudoku are examples that can also be beneficial so long as they remain complex and novel.

- Consider using brain-fitness software like that found on fitbrains.com. There are so many ways to engage and stimulate your mind—explore different brain-fitness software to find what works the best for you and your family.
- While at home, make it a habit to debate and discuss national and world events. Encourage everyone to speak.
- Encourage music, including playing an instrument and listening to music together.
- Learn a different language, including sign language.
- Read together and share the meaning of the story. Having critical discussions is a great way to engage your mind.

The home is always a great place to begin thinking about changes to promote a brain health culture where we live. Similar to the home setting, the work setting becomes an important environment to consider simply because we spend so much time at work.

Mental Stimulation in the Workplace

Similar to the home setting, the workplace is an environment where most of us spend a significant amount of time. It is probably true that many companies and work settings have wellness programs, such as walking clubs and nutritional advice programs. The work setting can also be an environment that provides opportunities for mental stimulation. It is important to first review your own behavior in the workplace and to assess how you might be able to derive more mental stimulation during your typical workday.

Most employees complete work duties on a daily basis that tend to be predictable and routinized. As such, employees spend a good deal of their time stimulating their subcortex, the part of the brain that helps with procedures and skills that require processing that is subconscious. The goal of a brain health environment is to provide novel and complex stimuli that engage and stimulate the cortex, help to build brain reserve, and maintain conscious processing. Consider the following for ways you can stimulate your brain at work:

- As an employee, you are encouraged to try new tasks and activities in your work setting. This will increase processing of stimuli that are novel and complex and increase the chance for brain health benefit.
- Do not be afraid to express your creative ideas and provide time for employees to imagine. Integration of diverse disciplines can help to forge new ideas that otherwise might tend to remain in operational silos.
- When leading a meeting, consider setting the chairs of the room in a circle or several small circles rather than rows and columns. This can engage everyone in a more integrated rather than didactic manner. A more integrated approach can promote personal interaction and constructive dialogue.

- Ask human resources if your company provides any assistance for you to enroll in formal lifelong learning that might occur at a local college or university or within the work setting itself.
- Ask if you can assume roles that will nurture your communication skills, including public speaking and provision of succinct responses that are both clear and informative. Ask your information officer if the company has technologies to assist your own daily tasks and if you can learn about the different software.
- Ask if you can establish a type of brain health kiosk in the work setting where employees can access information on the basics of the human brain and the brain health lifestyle, complete their online brain fitness workout, get the latest research news on the human brain and brain health, and even complete their online brain health survey to assess the strengths and weaknesses of their brain health lifestyle.

Mental Stimulation in Other Areas of Your Life

You can take a brief inventory of the environments you typically traverse on a daily basis. Most of us spend a healthy portion of our time at home, which is why a previous section was dedicated to mental stimulation in the home. However, we also spend time in other settings, such as our work site and maybe a gymnasium, library, or facilities where we recreate or enjoy entertainment. Once you have a conscious sense of where you typically spend your time, you can analyze the value of novelty and complexity that each environment provides you. The goal is to expose your brain to settings that provide activities and stimulation that are novel and complex. You can do this and still have some fun along the way! The following brain-health-promoting tips can be used in different areas of your life to promote mental stimulation:

- Try new tasks and activities in your daily life. Some ideas would be to accomplish your typical daily tasks using a different approach, or maybe you could reach your destination using a different route. By changing your approach, you will be providing your brain with novelty and complexity and therefore boost your brain health benefit.
- Try to develop one or two new hobbies over the next year. A hobby really is the development of a new talent, and this requires stimulating your brain to develop the neural circuitry that enables you to perform the task or hobby. You can learn how to use a new computer program, or you can take up golf or tennis, gardening or knitting. So long as the new activity is new for you, your brain will be stimulated in a healthy way.
- As the brain is pleased with multiple and simultaneous stimuli, consider and encourage communication and learning or teaching that engages multiple sensory systems. We all tend to rely heavily on our visual and auditory systems

to the neglect of our ability to taste, smell, and touch. Your brain can be stimulated using all the sensory pathways.

• Break out of intellectual silos and share knowledge. Perhaps most important from the perspective of brain health is the need to integrate and merge different bodies of knowledge, academic and applied, to form an entirely new intellectual or tangible entity (intellectual alloy). This is accomplished by getting groups of people to think differently and to merge their talents and knowledge with those of others. Most of the time we operate in silos with complete focus on our own goals and deadlines. We can enhance brain health and promote creativity, imagination, and innovation by breaking down silos and merging the content within the silos—the benefit being that mental stimulation, creativity, and new answers to old problems can emerge from this sharing of knowledge.

These are just a few tips to get you started—there are so many ways to engage your mind. Mental stimulation is critical to brain health. Your brain is constantly seeking and processing information. The wonderful thing about the human brain is that it changes and responds to the types of environmental input provided. This fact provides all of us the opportunity to select specific settings or environments that provide the most brain-health-promoting stimuli, so immerse yourself in enriched environments to keep your brain sharp and fit.

TIPS TO PROMOTE BRAIN HEALTH: QUICK REVIEW

- Keep an active reading habit. This can include a book or two a month, reading the newspaper every day, and a favorite magazine on a weekly basis.
- Enroll in a brain fitness program like those found on fitbrains.com. You can engage in daily activities that stimulate memory, language, attention, visuospatial, and executive skills.
- Engage in new activities that are challenging. Try to learn a new language or learn how to play a new instrument.
- Be artistic and creative. Pick up a hobby like painting, making pottery, or any other activity that promotes your imagination.
- Enroll in a class or workshop that interests you, perhaps a class on public speaking or even course offerings available through corporate learning centers.

8

CRITICAL AREA 4: SPIRITUALITY

I turned inward and became one with my world.

◉

Spirituality is another critical area that promotes brain health, and at first you may be skeptical, but in this chapter, I will show you how spirituality is directly connected to a healthier brain. When I talk about spirituality, I'm not necessarily addressing religion but rather engagement in deep introspection or meditation as part of the human condition. Although spirituality can be both formal, religiously inspired, as well as informal, using modes of introspection gained from such things as meditation, spirituality in the context of a brain health lifestyle is broadly defined as action or behavior that helps us slow down, turn inward, and rid our bodies of toxic stress.

Since the beginning of time, humans have engaged in behaviors we refer to as religion or spirituality or a belief in a higher power. For many years this reality has been resisted, wars continue to be fought over such matters, and deep intrapersonal conflict revolves around spirituality. I believe that we should not deny this reality but rather embrace it as part of our DNA and ask questions about whether and how spirituality can enhance our human condition and, in the case of this book, our brain health.

Encouraging Research That Connects Brain Health and Spirituality

I am not the only one who is interested in spirituality and the human brain, as an entire new field called "neurotheology" has developed to study this exact topic. To date, scientists have reported that prayer, which can be considered a form of meditation, on a daily basis enhances the immune system. The brains of monks in deep meditation as measured by PET (positron-emission tomography) scans, which measure levels of glucose metabolism, evince change as if there is no distinction between processing of what is going on outside the human brain from inside. This has potential significance as our brain typically differentiates processing information and activity that occurs inside versus outside of our brain. It appears from the PET scans that deep meditation removes the internal versus external processing and instead integrates the internal and external into a unified existence. Perhaps this is why those who meditate describe a peaceful existence. Persons who attend formalized religious service report happier lives and have healthier lives, and over 90 percent of American physicians report that prayer is important to the well-being of their patients. This is certainly a good start on trying to understand the relationship between our spirituality and health. With continued research, we will learn more and perhaps even have the courage to prescribe spiritual behaviors as part of our overall treatment regimen for patients in need.

Other research within the field of neurotheology has focused on the structural and functional relationship between our recognition of God and the human brain. I have seen reports that suggest our temporal and parietal lobes are primary sites for the relationship, but this is not conclusive. We know that temporal lobe epilepsy, in which a person will experience abnormal electrical activity within the cells of the temporal lobe, is associated with hyperreligiosity and even delusions of grandeur in which one may believe he or she is God. Research is ongoing to understand this relationship between God and brain so we can better explain why and how humans seek a higher being and how that impacts the function of the brain and our overall condition.

I have noticed that most people are a bit timid when talking about spirituality, but as I mentioned earlier, spirituality does not necessarily always go hand in hand with religious beliefs. Spirituality has many meanings, and it may mean something different to you than me. This section refers to spirituality as one means of turning inward to foster a peaceful existence and to remove oneself from the hurried society. Sometimes spirituality takes the form of engaging in prayer, meditation, and other relaxation procedures.

STRESS: IMPLICATIONS FOR BRAIN HEALTH

Why is it so important for humans and for the human brain to not be hurried, overwhelmed, rushed, or stressed? We all know how bad it feels when we're hurried or stressed, which also negatively affects us emotionally or behaviorally; what's also important to realize is this kind of anxiety affects our brain health as well. When our body and brain are at ease, we can achieve a relaxed state of being, one that enables our brain and body to perform at their most efficient level. Ridding our body and brain of the daily bombardment of stress and reaching a type of inner homeostasis is important, but difficult to achieve.

The Importance of Balance

Homeostasis is a term that refers to balance, symmetry, and smoothness that exists within our body. Our brains also experience homeostasis, which is a blissful state without anxiety, stress, or feeling rushed or troubled. We all feel this bliss at times, though it may be fleeting and temporary. More often, we experience a lack of homeostasis, and there can be significant negative consequences to our health and even our longevity if this imbalance becomes chronic. Disorders such as hypertension, obesity, addiction, depression, anxiety, somatic conditions, interpersonal tension, impulsivity, and even criminal behavior can relate to or even be caused by chronic stress and lack of balance in our minds.

We need to seek this homeostatic state by engaging in relaxation techniques such as prayer or meditation to reduce stress and achieve a balanced mind. This is as true for everybody from the person who works at home to the typical business professional all the way to an executive of a powerful company. Often we ignore this effort because we live in a fast-paced and demanding world that limits our ability to achieve such balance. It is important to first recognize the importance of balance, the fact that you are often in too big a hurry and too stressed, and to respect the negative health consequences of losing balance and homeostasis. Once you understand this, you can begin to make a conscious effort to identify behaviors in your own lifestyle that reduce your balance and to make the necessary changes for your health and brain health.

Research: Highly Stressed Environments Lead to Memory Loss

Animal research has found that rodents raised in an environment that is too stimulating demonstrate slowed brain development. In addition, animals exposed to environments that are highly stressful, where they have *little control*, demonstrate structural damage in their hippocampus and evince memory problems.

Early research on the human brain exposed to life-threatening stressors indicates there is a similar effect on the hippocampus.

Also, humans with chronic anxiety often have memory problems, which supports the theory that stress and uncontrolled anxiety have a negative effect on brain function. Research has even shown that chronic stress that can emerge from poverty in childhood has been related to increased risk of Alzheimer's disease later in life. In other words, stress can have both an acute and long-term effect on the body and brain. The point of this research, human and animal, is that we humans should take pause and examine how fast we are moving on a daily basis and decide if we need to slow down.

With chronic stress, some organisms undergo a type of sustained hormonal explosion; a proliferation of steroid hormones will infiltrate the brain of animals and perhaps humans. These steroid hormones are thought to be primarily responsible for the structural damage to the hippocampus and the negative consequence of memory loss and forgetfulness. Humans with post-traumatic stress disorder (PTSD) experience a therapeutic benefit from ongoing psychotherapy, and their cognition can return to near normal or even normal with successful therapy. This indicates that the potential damage from chronic stress can be reversed and further highlights the power of neural plasticity and brain health.

PROMOTE BRAIN HEALTH
THROUGH SPIRITUALITY

The goal of stress reduction can be accomplished, but it is not easy. We do need to be educated on the effects of stress on our body and brain, identify our own behaviors that contribute to increased stress and loss of balance, and then make changes in our lifestyle to promote balance. This is a lifelong battle, and it can be difficult, particularly in any culture that teaches "the quick fix." Three good behaviors to learn and to implement for achieving a healthier spirituality include prayer, meditation, and deep relaxation. Each of these three behaviors involves turning inward from the chaotic outside pressures and stress and reaching a type of internal peace. This can help to achieve the homeostasis and balance necessary for brain health described earlier.

Research and surveys have reported the following positive effects of prayer on health:

1. Prayer on a daily basis relates to an enhanced immune system, the system that helps you defend against colds, flu, and other illnesses.
2. Those who attend a formalized place of worship live longer and report happier and healthier lives than those who do not. Unfortunately, surveys suggest only 30 percent of people in the United States attend a formalized place of worship weekly.

3. Prayer (or meditation) as part of the daily routine while in the hospital relates to an earlier discharge. I would think the health care payer system would find this interesting!

BRAIN HEALTH TIP

Consider incorporating meditation, other relaxation techniques such as breathing exercises, or even prayer into your daily health routine.

Meditation and Relaxation Exercises

Meditation, relaxation procedures that include deep breathing, and progressive muscle relaxation are important to brain health. Unfortunately, we tend to use Band-Aid approaches, and we really do not fix the underlying problems or struggles of our lives. It is fair to say that a high number of "conditions" suffered by humans are stress-related and can probably be cured by changing certain lifestyle behaviors and by discovering the underlying cause of the stress and remedying it through spiritual introspection.

Meditation. Meditation can help you to slow down and turn inward for balance and symmetry. Your brain can adapt to a chaotic world, but it will function more efficiently over a longer period of time if you provide moments of inward reflection and rest. Meditation offers one technique to achieve such inner peace, and Western cultures are now more accepting of meditation and yoga.

Part of your brain health program can include a lesson or two on meditation so you can engage in this behavior on a daily basis. Fortunately, other cultures have already embraced the power of meditation and the benefits derived from deep introspection. The growing popularity of meditation makes it easier to find various kinds of guided meditation techniques online like how-to-meditate.org.

Breathing Exercises. Similarly, you may not know how to breathe correctly or to use breathing techniques to rid your body of stress. You are encouraged to engage in proper relaxation breathing exercises two to three times daily. Taking a deep inhalation through your nose using your stomach muscles and holding the breath for several seconds will result in your feeling some tension in your stomach and chest. Now, slowly release the air using your stomach and pushing the air out of your mouth in a rhythmic way. Doing this exercise several times for a few minutes throughout the day can help you to slow down and gain a sense of calm as you rid yourself of toxic stress.

Listen to Your Body's Stress Indicators. It is important not only to identify the stressors in your life but also to understand and locate what part of your body is vulnerable to stress. You may experience stress in your neck, lower back, head, or stomach. By identifying what part of your body stress targets, you can then engage in progressive muscle relaxation procedures to alleviate the stress from your target site. For example, squeeze your right hand into a fist as hard as you can. Hold the fist and pay attention to how uncomfortable the tension is in your fist.

Now, slowly release your fingers, extending them, and notice how the tension leaves your fingers. The more relaxed feeling achieved by letting the fist go and extending your fingers is an example of how you can focus on any muscle group in your body to release stress. Tightening and releasing muscles all over your body (head to toe) two to three times a day will provide much-needed relief from tension. At the end of the exercise, you will notice that energy in the form of stress has left you, and you will feel better!

BRAIN HEALTH TIP

Practice progressive muscle relaxation and deep breathing exercises two to three times daily. Turning inward will help your brain escape temporarily the stress-filled and unenriched environments of life.

Spirituality at Home

You will benefit from slowing down, relaxation, and developing inner balance, and practicing at home would probably be your best bet. Like everyone else, you and your family are hurried and many times neglect to take a moment of reflection. Make your home an escape where you can engage with reflective meditation and spirituality. Chronic stress builds up from a hurried environment and can do structural and functional damage to our brains. Spirituality offers some practical methods to slow down. Here are some ways you can explore spirituality at home to promote brain health:

- Create a space for yourself at home, either designating a specific room or a specific area of your home office or living room as a place to meditate, pray, or practice breathing and progressive muscle relaxation. Allotting a specific area makes you more likely to practice reflective meditation and spirituality on a daily basis.

- Create a special time, whether it's for ten or fifteen minutes a day, to just sit in silence, away from technology, with the goal of slowing down. You can take this block of time to meditate, pray, or reflect. You could even take a walk in the park or around the block, go on a short bike ride, or do some other quiet activity that puts your mind at ease—encourage your family to do the same.

- Attend a formalized place of worship on a regular basis, as this has been shown to be connected to happiness and longevity. If this is not an activity that is possible for you or your family, consider the other methods of spirituality described in this chapter.

- Keep a box of cards that have meditative reflections around the house. The moment you begin to feel anxious or stressed, stop and take a moment to relax and go through some of the meditative reflections.

Chronic stress can be damaging to the body and to the brain, particularly to functions such as memory and mood. We know that animals that are exposed to environments that are too stimulating experience slowed brain development. We also know that relaxation, slowing down, enjoying the moment, gaining homeostasis, and engaging in formal and informal spirituality can lead to better general health and to brain health. Now that you have some ideas for how you and your family can be spiritual at home, it is important to also apply some of these tips at work.

Spirituality in the Workplace

Every day you're encouraged to do more to meet deadlines, produce more, be more innovative—to be better, faster, and stronger. It's no wonder that the workforce is stressed and burned out. This chronic stress, as I've mentioned earlier, is detrimental to brain health, which is why now, more than ever, we need to cultivate and create a brain-health-conscious culture at work. You need to slow down and achieve inner balance— even at work. Here are some practical ways to boost spirituality at work:

- Engage in a quiet moment of daily prayer, meditation, and simply closing your eyes when you're commuting on your way to work.
- Consider your lunch break as a time for you to either meditate or focus on reflective spirituality—find a quiet place away from your desk and away from distractions. Giving yourself thirty minutes each day to slow down and turn to a spiritual activity will help rid your body of stress and enable more efficient brain function.

- Ask your human resources department if there are wellness programs available, such as yoga or meditation classes that offer corporate discounts.
- Engage in two or three five-minute periods throughout the day to engage in breathing exercises or muscle relaxation techniques.

Promote Spirituality in Other Areas of Your Life

It is really important for us to achieve homeostasis and balance, particularly when we are confronted by such a rapid pace in daily life. We have already discussed why spirituality is important to general and brain health and how we can express our spirituality at home and in the workplace. We can now consider how we might apply spiritual behaviors in other settings that we encounter as part of our normal lives. Spirituality provides all of us techniques to slow down, turn inward, reduce the negative physiological effects of chronic stress on our brain and body, and help us to generate a more pleasing sense of balance and homeostasis. Consider these additional tips and ideas for you to express formal and informal spirituality in your daily life:

- Visit your favorite setting two to three times a week. This might be a community park, lake, beach, mountain base, river, or anywhere you feel at peace. Enjoy the beauty of your environment—taking in the beauty of your surroundings can also be considered spiritual.

- Get outside or simply remove your body and mind from the tasks that are in front of you. Everything else will be waiting for you when you return.
- Sometimes music helps when you retreat to your spiritual place. I like to download sounds of the ocean and waves and listen to soothing music while I pray or meditate.

It is both important for us to change our lifestyles and learn to slow down to promote brain health. Engaging in spirituality is a great way to stop, reflect, meditate, and relax to take a respite from our hurried lifestyles. While that is easily said and understood, it is also very difficult to change behavior. In order for you to achieve success with the spiritual domain as part of the brain health lifestyle, you must first identify the stress in your life, where you experience stress in your body, and how you deal with this stress now. To deal with your stress effectively, consider the tips provided you in this chapter and encourage your family do the same.

Tips to Promote Brain Health: Quick Review

- Learn relaxation procedures that include rhythmic breathing and progressive muscle relaxation.
- Forms of spirituality such as meditation, relaxation procedures, enjoying nature, yoga, and tai chi can help you turn inward and remove stress from your body.
- Give yourself thirty minutes a day every day for your own quiet time to be reflective.
- Keep guided meditation cards or prayers at your fingertips for moments when you feel entirely overwhelmed. Keep a deck of these cards at home or in your office.
- Create a special area for yourself at home specifically for meditation or prayer.
- Get a good night's sleep so that you feel rested in the morning.

9

CRITICAL AREA 5: NUTRITION

What we eat shapes the structure and function of our brain, including thoughts and emotions.

◉

One of the most popular and studied areas of health care today is that of nutrition and how what we eat relates to our general well-being. This is particularly true for diet and the human brain. Indeed, an entire new field of study known as nutritional neurosciences has evolved to address this growing interest. Today we believe that the foods we consume not only affect our general body but can also affect our emotion, thoughts, energy level, and even our ability to have a healthy brain later in life. In this chapter, I'll show you how you can eat for the benefit of a healthier brain. Later on I'll also give you some great recipes so you can easily incorporate nutrition into your healthy brain lifestyle.

How the Food You Eat Affects Brain Health

As humans, we've been shaped to some degree by the types of foods we have eaten. Our bodies and behavior will be shaped literally by the types of food, good or bad, that we consume, and this has been the case for thousands of years. Nearly everything we put in our mouths is converted into glucose and absorbed into the cells of our body for energy. As the brain is most demanding and will take nearly 25 percent of the energy from each swallow, there is a direct relationship to what we eat and the structural and functional integrity of our brain.

Perhaps as important is the fact that the brain consists of nearly 60 percent fat and may actually be the fattest part of our bodies. The fat in our brain is really a lipid substance that insulates our nerve tracts and cells and helps the brain process information rapidly. When the fat breaks down, we tend not to think efficiently, we may experience attention problems, and we may suffer emotional changes such as sadness. It is important for everyone to understand that by keeping a robust level of fat in our brains, we are actually helping to shape our brains toward health.

Our diet provides us a direct pathway to build up the fat in our brains. We have access to foods that contain good fats, those typically found in fatty fish, such as salmon, herring, mackerel, and sardines. Some unsalted nuts, such as almonds and walnuts, also have good, or healthy, fats. These types of healthy fats help the brain function more efficiently and are characterized as omega-3 fatty acids. Bad, or unhealthy, fats are found in foods high in trans-fatty acids or saturated fats. These unhealthy fats can do damage to the brain over time and are commonly found in fast foods and fried foods, among others. We need to try and achieve as high a ratio of healthy fats to unhealthy fats as we can. Unfortunately, our current ratios, as a nation, are quite poor.

Today a typical person, particularly those who live in westernized cultures, will consume nearly fifteen times more bad fat than good fat. This is a significantly unhealthy balance that increases the risk of brain dysfunction from a variety of disorders, such as cerebrovascular disease, cardiovascular disease, obesity, and diabetes. Intake of bad fats, including trans-fatty acids, saturated fats, and omega-6 fatty acids, can lead to a breakdown in the plasticity of brain cells, creating less efficient information processing.

The significant rise in obesity and diabetes during the past twenty-five years reveals how high-fat and processed foods have literally changed our appearance and increased our health problems. Unhealthy foods have also contributed to increases in mental illness, sleep disorders, dementia, stroke, and even attention deficit disorder. If this is true and some foods can actually alter our neurochemistry toward dysfunction and disease, other foods can also promote brain health. It becomes important to identify and adopt a specific diet, not just for our well-being but also for brain health!

Ancestral Diets: Eating Fish Nurtures the Brain

According to some, our earliest ancestors followed a simple diet that *did* promote brain health. The diet included leaves, plants, berries, nuts, beans, fish, and lean game. Estimates indicate that our prehistoric ancestors consumed one good fat for every bad fat, an extremely healthy balance of fat intake. Remember, your brain is 60 percent fat, and this lipid needs to be nurtured by consumption of healthy fats for proper and efficient processing of information.

Did you know that human civilizations had their greatest periods of development when living and working near water? One reason may be that the water provided for a greater consumption of fatty fish, which contains the good fat that nurtures the brain and permits the brain to be at its functional and intellectual best. Consider all the great achievements of our early ancestors who lived near the Euphrates and Nile Rivers and the Mediterranean Sea. Consumption of proper fats typically found in fatty fish promotes flexibility in brain cells and efficient transmission of information between cells. It helps the cell membrane maintain a type of elasticity rather than a rigid and fixed state that will reduce information processing. Once again, the brain is highly lipid, with nearly 60 percent of the brain composed of fat. Foods that help to maintain the healthy levels of lipid and fat in the brain are enormously helpful to the structural and functional integrity of the brain.

From the Agricultural Revolution to Processed Foods

As we evolved, the agricultural revolution brought diets containing milk, eggs, cheese, and meat. These foods are not considered brain-healthy even though they have become standard in most diets. With the beginning of the industrial and now information revolution, diets have included new foods known as processed foods. The entire fast-food industry was born, and today it provides a major part of millions of persons' daily nutritional intake. Processed foods are unhealthy—filled with bad fats, salt, sugars, and calories. Processed foods are a major contributor to the risk of obesity, diabetes, and a myriad of disorders that can result in degeneration and dysfunction of the human brain. Obesity and diabetes alone are major threats to the function of the brain, correlate with stroke and dementia, and now occur in childhood at unprecedented rates relative to any other time in our history.

Antioxidants and Brain Health

In addition to the brain-healthy effects of omega-3s in such foods as fatty fish, antioxidants have been shown to be wonderful for our general health and for brain health. Remember when you were a child and your parents and grandparents told you to "eat your vegetables"? It turns out they were pretty smart, because it is precisely the fruits and vegetables that have high antioxidant properties and are very healthy for our brains.

An antioxidant is a type of "broom" that helps to sweep the toxins out of our bodies. Believe it or not, our bodies are filled with toxins known as "free radicals" that can cause or lead to many disorders from cataracts, arthritis, cancer, heart disease, osteoporosis, and even dementia. It is paradoxical, because free radicals begin in the oxygen molecules that we need to survive. It seems that the oxygen molecule becomes unstable electrically and breaks away to bond with another cell in the body. This "free" roaming and binding of the cell causes the damage "radical" that can lead to the conditions just mentioned. We believe free radicals develop from pollution, chronic stress, too much wear and tear on the body, toxins, and even poor diet. As our bodies do not produce many antioxidants as we get older, we need to supplement our levels through the diet. This is where fruits and vegetables become critical, because they are filled with antioxidants that can help to fight against free radicals.

It is vital to appreciate the importance of food and nutrition in our lives. Food has a biological and a social importance to us. We can work to increase the amount of healthy foods and also have some fun. Food provides us a great opportunity to socialize, network, recreate, and enjoy intimate moments. Food is also a pleasure and really needs to be enjoyed. I have asked Kathy Rusk, a registered dietician, to help with the next section of this chapter. Kathy will help us to learn more about the specific foods that are good for our brain, and at the end of the chapter, she even provides us with some brain-healthy recipes that we can try in our own kitchens. For more information and nutritional tips, visit her website: nutritiondynamicsnw.com.

HEALTHY BRAIN DIET

A healthy human brain relies on having a mixture of nutrients from a variety of foods. Macronutrients (carbohydrates, protein, and fats) and micronutrients (vitamins and minerals) are vital for the human brain to function at all, and preferably well, throughout life. However, we know now that specific nutrients within these categories have a greater effect on the functioning of the brain than others. As we've seen, some fats should be avoided, others lowered, and some even increased.

Scientists now know that there are hundreds if not thousands of micronutrients in specific foods that are high in the particular nutrients that the brain needs. In order to have a well-functioning brain, consume a variety of foods that provide the nutrients that a healthy brain needs. No one food is magically going to improve the brain's function; instead there are many foods to include in a typical day and week. Consuming nutrients in their natural form is the safest and surest way to meet nutritional needs for a healthy brain.

Carbohydrates yield energy that provides fuel for the brain for short-term memory and basic thinking skills. Therefore, as an energy source, any carbohydrate is effective. However, it behooves one to consume them in foods that have a low glycemic index, those that contain low levels of fructose, and foods that carry with them beneficial nutrients.

Protein makes up neurotransmitters that allow the brain cells to communicate; they are the building blocks of the brain's network. Protein is also a component of the myelin sheath that covers neurons. Complete proteins are essential for these components. The human body is able to synthesize all the proteins needed from nitrogen-containing foodstuff (amino acids) consumed in various foods, as long as the essential amino acids, those the body cannot produce by itself, are consumed.

Fats make up 70 percent of the protective myelin sheath that covers the neurons responsible for the communication within the brain; DHA (docosahexaenoic acid) is the specific omega-3 fatty acid that is especially important for this myelin sheath, and thus for brain health. Look ahead to the "Fats" section for foods high in DHA.

Micronutrients contain antioxidants that act in extraordinary synergy with each other to neutralize the free radicals that are produced in the brain that could damage the brain cells faster than they can be repaired. Antioxidants that benefit the brain specifically are in a variety of food.

Carbohydrates

Carbohydrates have been categorized into a glycemic index, which is a tool to quantify the amount that will cause blood sugars to rise. High blood-sugar levels, if not reduced by a normal insulin response, are harmful to some organs, including the brain. In general, the more processed a carbohydrate is, the more quickly blood sugar will rise. However, the glycemic load in one food item can vary depending on its ripeness, how long it is cooked, the actual temperature of the food, the acidity of the specific food at that time and what it is eaten with, and the volume of food consumed while eating this carbohydrate. The effect can differ for individuals as well, as a person's metabolism can vary from day to day. Nevertheless, the general rule is that the higher the glycemic load in a meal, the higher the likelihood that insulin will increase and can result in a negative situation of high blood-sugar levels in the body and brain. Such high levels of blood sugar predispose the body to diabetes and increased risk for brain dysfunction from stroke, hypertension, and dementia.

Fructose, a component of the polysaccharide glucose, by itself has been shown recently to have a deleterious effect on insulin's utilization within the body. More research is needed, but knowing that pure glucose is not in itself advantageous except for calories, "added fructose" is considered by many to be ill-advised. However, the glucose, and thus fructose too, in fruits and vegetables, which are surrounded by many important antioxidants, are not to be equated with pure added sugars in food. Why? Because fruits and vegetables are the main sources of micronutrients, a separate category, which I'll tell you about later on.

Specific sources of carbohydrates to include in your brain health diet:

- Rye grain
- Other whole grains with fiber
- Oats
- Dried beans and lentils
- Nuts
- Barley

Protein

Getting adequate protein is essential for a healthy brain. However, proteins in food are often accompanied with fat. In general, the higher-quality proteins, which are considered complete proteins and have all amino acids present, are from animal sources, whereas lower-quality proteins, lacking some or significant amounts of essential amino acids, generally come from plant sources. However, plant sources can complement each other when eaten in combination. Examples are legumes with grains, nuts, or seeds. Also, grains, low in one amino acid, are complemented well when consumed with milk, which is higher than other foods in the specific amino acid that most grains are lower in. Soybeans, in themselves, provide complete proteins. Specific proteins that are considered beneficial for brain health are found in the following:

- **Fish.** Those with the omega-3 fatty acids, such as salmon, mackerel, herring, sardines, and some trout are particularly beneficial.
- **Fowl.** Turkey and chickens are especially beneficial when raised on algae-based chicken feed.
- **Lean beef and pork.** These animals, as well as buffalo, are excellent sources of good protein when the meat is lean and the animal has been range-fed.
- **Eggs.** Chickens fed feed with DHA added produce a more brain-healthy egg, but an egg, in itself, is beneficial. There is an ongoing debate about whether the cholesterol in eggs

is really bad for you, but now some scientists believe that the harm from the cholesterol in eggs has been overstated.

- **Dairy products.** Low-fat or fat-free milk, cheese, and other products are excellent sources of complete protein.
- **Complementary foods.** Legumes with grains or nuts and seeds together provide the amino acids that the body can synthesize to make complete proteins.

Fats

Fats need special attention in the contemporary diet. The ideal diet would contain no or just slight amounts of trans fats; a small amount of saturated fat; acceptable levels of monounsaturated fats, since they have a neutral effect on the brain but can provide either desirable or undesirable calories; and polyunsaturated fats in specified amounts. The most frequently referenced polyunsaturated fats are in vegetables and grains, such as corn and soybean oils; omega-3 and omega-6 are polyunsaturated fats. The low intake of omega-3, and the possible overconsumption of omega-6 in relation to omega-3, can be detrimental to brain function. When omega-3 is in a good balance with omega-6, it is believed to be brain boosting. It is generally agreed that the ratio of omega-6 to omega-3 should be 4:1 or better.

Therefore, it's important to eat foods with less saturated fat. Minimal saturated fat in low-fat dairy products and small servings of red meat, chicken, or pork are acceptable. Consume no trans fats, or only the trans fats that are naturally in some meats. Do make an effort to include lower amounts of oils with omega-6 fatty acids (corn, safflower, palm, sunflower, and cottonseed oils). Soybean oil should be used in moderation. Olive oil has a neutral affect; canola oil is acceptable, with more omega-3s than any other oil and also less omega-6s. Include at least two servings per week of the foods that contain the fatty acid omega-3 DHA (docosahexaenoic acid):

- Salmon, wild, Pacific or Atlantic
- Herring
- Mackerel
- Sardines

Enjoy foods with ALA (alpha-linolenic acid). It is inefficiently converted to DHA but is needed in the body:

- Flaxseed oil
- Green leafy vegetables
- Walnuts
- Pumpkin seeds
- Hemp seeds or hemp seed oil

Foods with oleic acid (monounsaturated fats):

- Olive oil
- Almonds
- Peanuts
- Avocados

Micronutrients

A wide variety of fruits and vegetables should be included in a daily and weekly diet. The varieties of micronutrients necessary for optimum brain health are too frequently minimized; several cannot do the work of all. Hundreds of known antioxidants exist and play a role in a healthy brain; the possibly yet-to-be discovered other antioxidants that are in natural food will not appear in pills but most surely exist, according to some scientists.

As more research is done, more micronutrients are being found to be antioxidants, which protect the brain from free radicals that can and do damage brain cells. Antioxidants work together, and therefore, eating foods that contain a variety of them is the best way to make sure all of them are included. Here are some known high-antioxidant foods that are beneficial to the brain:

Blueberries
Blackberries
Kale
Walnuts
Brussels sprouts
Artichokes
Spinach
Beets
Green or black tea
Brewed coffee
Pecans

Grape juice
Dark leafy green vegetables
Dark chocolate
Strawberries
Unsweetened baking chocolate
Red grapes
Artichokes
Red wine
Elderberries
Cranberries
Oranges
Grapefruit
Apricots
Cherries
Garlic
Lentil, pinto, or black beans

What About Nutritional Supplements?

We are all similar in that many of us have tried hard to start a diet that is healthy for us, but we cannot maintain it. I know personally how hard this is even though I know eating a healthy diet is good for me. For those of us who are not getting enough fatty fish for our omega-3s every week—we need several ounces several times a week—or enough fruits and vegetables for our antioxidants, we need to try and make a conscious effort to increase these foods in our diet. If you're having trouble incorporating all of these brain-healthy foods into your diet, then you may need to consider nutritional supplements, though I am a big proponent of getting the proper vitamins and minerals organically.

I have found that supplements that have fish oil, like omega-3 pills, tend to be too big, have a fishy aftertaste, and are often processed with fillers. Fortunately, there's a new product on the market called Moxxor (moxxor.com/drpaul), which provides a powerful combination of several omega-3s with an antioxidant and without any filler. The nutritional product is small, it leaves no fishy aftertaste, and it is touted as one of the most powerful omega-3s available. Remember, it's always important to communicate any change in your diet to your physician before trying new nutritional supplements.

PROMOTE BRAIN HEALTH THROUGH NUTRITION

Food is a critical and necessary part of our lives—it sustains us and provides us with the necessary energy to lead a vibrant life. The critical issue becomes the quality and quantity of food that we eat. Including specific brain-healthy foods in your diet while staying away from trans-fatty acids, fast foods, processed foods, and too much sugar will place you on the path back to the brain health diet of our early ancestors.

We all need to become more conscious of our eating behavior, not only the quantity and quality of the foods we eat. This is a lifelong process, but changing eating habits from unhealthy to healthy can be very rewarding, help us feel better, think more clearly, and get our brains in better shape. In the section ahead, we'll look at how you can practice better nutrition for brain health at home, at work, and in other areas of your life.

Nutrition at Home

Everyone in the home can get involved in learning what foods promote brain health. Family members can have fun purchasing brain health foods and preparing meals together. Helping each family member choose brain-healthy foods and rewarding each other can be a good time. Trying new recipes and changing behavior to begin looking for such brain-healthy foods at grocery stores and restaurants only reinforces a healthy lifestyle. Consider the following ideas for nutrition and brain health in the home:

- Keep journals of what foods you eat throughout the day to ensure that you're eating enough brain-healthy foods.
- Keep a list on your refrigerator of the various brain-boosting foods you've learned about in this chapter. Doing this will encourage and remind you to purchase the specific kinds of brain foods at the grocery store.
- Keep a basket of fresh fruits that are filled with brain-boosting antioxidants in your kitchen.

Nutrition in the Workplace

In any work setting that has a cafeteria, it is relatively easy to implement brain health and nutrition for employees. Even without a cafeteria or formal setting to eat, employees can benefit from information on brain health and nutrition and brain-healthy recipes.

We now have adequate research to list specific foods that reduce the risk of dementia or promote brain health, and this information needs to be communicated everywhere, including workplace cafeterias. I believe all foods that are brain health promoting should have a little brain icon on their packaging to help the consumer make a brain-healthy choice. Consider the following to improve brain health nutrition in the workplace:

- Speak to some of your colleagues about starting a brain health awareness group.
- Ask your human resources department if you can work with some of your colleagues and the dietary staff to create a more brain-healthy environment in the cafeteria and lounge.
- Rather than bringing sweets and candies as a treat during meetings and events, consider bringing nuts and fruits instead.
- Bring your own lunch, with more fruits and vegetables, and consider bringing fish that you can prepare in the office pantry.

Other Ways to Promote Nutrition

We have become what we eat, with literal changes in our DNA and genetic makeup over time. Interestingly, from a brain health perspective, we were really never meant to eat meat, cheese, eggs, milk, and certainly not the processed foods that were invented with the industrial age. We really are supposed to eat lean meats, fruit, vegetables, fish, nuts, and beans. Along the way, we have incurred the consequences of such a dramatic dietary change in the form of heart disease, diabetes, obesity, stroke, and probably many other serious diseases. Consider the following ideas to promote brain health nutrition in your life:

- Consider working with a few local restaurants and even your grocery store to develop a section of the menu or the store where foods that have high brain health value are labeled with a little brain icon. This would help to educate the consumer.
- Consider taking a course on nutrition to learn more about brain health and diet.
- Consider keeping a journal for two weeks of what you eat on a daily basis. This can help you become conscious of what you are eating and perhaps why you eat certain foods. You might be surprised how much easier it is to incorporate more brain-healthy foods into your diet.

Eating is one our most pleasurable and enjoyable activities. We are not very different from other animals, though we may enjoy the psychology and intimacy of food more than animals.

We all need food to survive, and this section attempts to outline the importance of a brain healthy diet. Following is a recap of some basic points to consider if you intend to change your diet to benefit your brain.

TIPS TO PROMOTE BRAIN HEALTH: QUICK REVIEW

- Increase your fish intake every week, especially fatty fish, such as salmon, herring, mackerel, sardines, and tuna, as these foods are rich in omega-3 fatty acids, which is a healthy brain fat.
- Eat five servings of fruits and vegetables a day. Fruits and vegetables are rich with antioxidants, which have properties that promote brain health by helping to rid our bodies of toxins known as free radicals. Green, leafy vegetables along with tomatoes are high in antioxidants.
- Use canola oil and olive oil when cooking. These oils are considered best, as they are less processed than other oils, such as corn oil, and contain ingredients that are converted into long-chain omega-3s that are great for the brain.
- Eat more unsalted nuts, especially walnuts, as they are rich in omega-3 fatty acids.
- Eating proper carbohydrates, like whole grains, oats, and rye grain, provides your brain with fuel for the short-term memory and basic thinking skills.

SOUPS

Tomato Soup with Basil
Serves 6

3 cloves garlic
1½ cups fresh basil
2 tablespoons olive oil
4 pounds very ripe tomatoes
1 teaspoon sugar
½ onion, diced
1 celery stem, diced
2 tablespoons chopped parsley
2 tablespoons chopped cilantro
2 cups chicken broth
Salt and pepper to taste
Parmesan cheese, optional

Blend the garlic, basil, and olive oil. Set aside. Put the tomatoes in very hot water for 1 minute and then gently peel off the skin. Place into a soup pot. Add the blended garlic, basil, and oil, and then add the sugar, onion, celery, parsley, and cilantro, setting aside a few sprigs of the cilantro to use as garnish. Simmer for about half an hour or until the tomato mixture has been reduced to three-fourths of its original volume. Add broth to taste. Add salt and pepper if necessary. Serve hot or cold, and garnish with cilantro sprigs. Optional: if served hot, sprinkle with grated Parmesan cheese.

One serving—Calories: 140; Total fat: 6 g; Total carbohydrates: 19 g; Protein: 4 g; Sodium: 360 mg

Butternut Squash Soup
Serves 12

5 cups canned chicken broth
4 cups fresh butternut squash, cubed
1 cup potato, unpeeled and diced
1 cup Vidalia onion, chopped
1 tablespoon garlic cloves, minced
1 teaspoon gingerroot, minced
½ cup light cream
¼ cup fresh orange juice
1 tablespoon fresh lemon juice
1 teaspoon salt
1 teaspoon hot chili sauce

Put the chicken broth and then the squash, potato, onion, garlic, and ginger into a large soup pot with a lid and set over medium heat. Bring to a boil, reduce the heat, cover, and simmer for about 45 minutes, until the vegetables are very soft. Take the mixture and puree, then whisk in the cream, orange and lemon juice, salt, and chili sauce. Reheat but do not boil.

One serving—Calories: 150; Total fat 8 g; Total carbohydrates: 16 g; Protein: 3 g; Sodium: 830 mg

SAUCES AND DIPS

Hummus
Serves 16

1 can (15 ounces) chickpeas (garbanzo beans),
   undrained
2 tablespoons fresh lemon juice
4 tablespoons tahini
4–6 cloves garlic
¼ teaspoon salt
4 drops Tabasco or to taste

Drain the chickpeas, reserving ¼ cup of the liquid. Rinse the
chickpeas. In a blender or food processor, blend all the ingredients together, including the reserved liquid. Serve with vegetable sticks, crackers, or bread.

One serving (2 tablespoons)—Calories: 45; Total fat: 2.5 g;
Total carbohydrates: 5 g; Protein: 2 g; Sodium: 65 mg

Yogurt-Herb Dipping Sauce
Serves 16

¾ cup plain yogurt
⅓ cup sour cream
1½ teaspoons fresh parsley, chopped
1½ teaspoons fresh cilantro, chopped
1½ teaspoons green onion, chopped
½ teaspoon celery salt

In a mixing bowl, combine the yogurt, sour cream, parsley, cilantro, green onion, and celery salt. Mix well, cover, and refrigerate for a minimum of 1 hour before serving.

One serving (1 tablespoon)—Calories: 15; Total fat: 1 g; Total carbohydrates: 1 g; Protein: 1 g; Sodium: 40 mg

Chilled Curry Cream
Serves 6

2 tablespoons salted butter
1 tablespoon curry powder
1 cup sour cream

In a small skillet, melt the butter over low heat; whisk in the curry powder and cook gently on low heat for 1 minute to flavor the butter. Turn off the heat and whisk in the cream. Chill. Chilled curry cream goes very well with soups!

One serving (3 tablespoons)—Calories: 90; Total fat: 12 g; Total carbohydrates: 3 g; Protein: 1.5 g; Sodium: 97mg

Peanut Sauce
Serves 9

1 cup natural creamy peanut butter
⅛ cup soy sauce
¼ cup lemon juice
2 cloves garlic, minced
1 teaspoon red pepper flakes
1 teaspoon sugar
2 tablespoons sherry
1 tablespoon sesame oil

Combine all ingredients and 1 cup hot water in a blender. Process until smooth. Store in refrigerator. Serve on Salmon Rama or other fish.

One serving (4½ tablespoons)—Calories: 190; Total fat: 16 g; Total carbohydrates: 9 g; Protein: 8 g; Sodium: 470 mg

Rémoulade Sauce
Serves 32

¼ cup creole mustard
2 tablespoons paprika
1 teaspoon cayenne pepper
1 cup green onions, chopped
½ cup celery, chopped
½ cup fresh parsley leaves
½ cup white vinegar
1⅓ cups olive oil
1 teaspoon prepared horseradish
¼ cup ketchup

Combine mustard, paprika, cayenne pepper, green onions, celery, parsley, and vinegar in a food processor. Turn processor on and let it run for about 2 minutes. Turn it off and scrape down the sides. Turn machine back on and let it run while slowly pouring in the olive oil, horseradish, and ketchup. Blend to make a smooth sauce. Serve on the Salmon Rémoulade Salad.

One serving (2 tablespoons)—Calories: 90; Total fat: 9 g; Total carbohydrates: 1 g; Protein: 0 g; Sodium: 45 mg

BEEF DISH

Stuffed Green Peppers
Serves 8

2 pounds ground range-fed beef
4 eggs
½ cup grated Parmesan cheese
2 cloves fresh garlic
1 cup Italian-style breadcrumbs
1 teaspoon Italian seasoning
½ cup cooked brown rice
4 large green peppers, sliced in half and seeded
2 cans tomato sauce
Salt and pepper to taste

Preheat oven to 350°F. Grease bottom of pan with olive oil. Mix meat, eggs, cheese, garlic, breadcrumbs, and Italian seasoning in large bowl. Add rice and mix together. Fill eight pepper halves with meat mixture. Place in pan and pour both cans of tomato sauce over top and along bottom of pan. Cook at 350°F for about 1 hour.

One serving—Calories: 380; Total fat: 20 g; Total carbohydrates: 20 g; Protein: 32 g; Sodium: 800 mg

Vegetarian Dishes

Vegetarian Dutch Baby
Serves 6

Vegetable cooking spray
1 cup shredded cabbage
2 ounces fresh mushrooms, sliced
2 large zucchini, thinly sliced
¾ cup onion, diced
½ cup each yellow, green, and red peppers, diced
4 cloves garlic, minced
¾ cup canned, cooked black beans, drained
    and rinsed
1 teaspoon dried whole basil
1 teaspoon dried whole thyme
⅛ teaspoon salt
⅛ teaspoon pepper
1 tablespoon butter
½ cup all-purpose flour
½ cup skim milk
2 eggs, beaten
1 cup (4 ounces) mozzarella cheese, shredded

Preheat the oven to 425°F. Coat a large nonstick skillet with
cooking spray; place over medium-high heat until hot. Add
cabbage, mushrooms, zucchini, onion, peppers, and garlic and
sauté 6 to 7 minutes or until vegetables are tender, stirring

frequently. Stir in black beans, basil, thyme, salt, and pepper. Remove from heat and keep warm.

Coat a 9-inch pie plate with cooking spray; add butter. Put in oven at 425°F for 1 minute or until butter melts. Combine flour, milk, and eggs in a medium bowl; stir well with wire whisk. Pour into prepared pie plate; do not stir.

Bake flour mixture at 425°F for 15 to 20 minutes or until puffed and browned. Spoon vegetable mixture into shell; sprinkle with cheese. Bake 1 to 2 minutes or until the cheese melts. Serve immediately.

One serving—Calories: 170; Total fat: 5 g; Total carbohydrates: 19 g; Protein: 12 g; Sodium: 350 mg

CHICKEN DISHES

Chicken with Mango Salsa
Serves 8

2 pounds chicken breasts, boneless and skinless

Mango Salsa
Makes 4 cups

> 2 ripe mangoes, peeled, pitted, and finely chopped
> 1 avocado, peeled, pitted, and cubed
> 1 red pepper, seeded and minced
> ½ cup cilantro, chopped with stems removed
> 2 green onions, minced
> 2 tablespoons ginger, finely minced
> 2 tablespoons orange juice, preferably freshly
> squeezed
> 2 tablespoons lime juice, preferably freshly squeezed
> 2 packed tablespoons brown sugar
> 1 teaspoon Asian chili sauce

Combine the mango salsa ingredients. Allow to sit for several hours at room temperature.

Grill the chicken on a barbecue or broil in under-oven broiler. Chicken is done when the juices are no longer pink. Serve the chicken with the mango sauce.

One serving—Calories: 190; Total fat: 5 g; Total carbohydrates: 9 g; Protein: 26 g; Sodium: 65 mg

Chicken, Broccoli, and Brown Rice Casserole
Serves 8

3 cups cooked brown rice
2 pounds broccoli, fresh or frozen
⅓ cup flour
1 teaspoon salt
⅛ teaspoon black pepper
1½ pounds chicken breasts, boneless and skinless
2 tablespoons salted butter
¾ cup white wine
1¼ cups chicken broth
1½ tablespoons brandy, 86 proof
1 cup grated Gouda cheese, optional

Prepare brown rice according to directions. Blanch fresh or frozen broccoli.

Preheat the oven to 350°F. Combine flour, salt, and pepper. Flatten the chicken breasts. Dredge with the flour mixture. Melt the butter in a medium to large sauté pan. Sauté the chicken breasts in the melted butter for 2 to 3 minutes. Remove from the pan and keep warm.

Stir the wine and chicken broth into the juices in the same pan. Reduce the liquid, add the brandy, and cook for 1 more minute.

Layer the brown rice, then the broccoli in a 3-quart casserole. Add the chicken and pour the wine sauce over the rice, broccoli, and chicken. Bake uncovered for 15 minutes or until light and bubbly. If using, sprinkle Gouda over chicken.

One serving—Calories: 290; Total fat: 6 g; Total carbohydrates: 29; Protein: 25 g; Sodium: 550 mg

Fish Dishes

Salmon Rama
Serves 3

1 can (14.75 ounces) wild Alaska pink salmon,
    drained, bones and skin removed
12 cups raw baby spinach leaves (will cook down to
    1½ cups cooked)
¾ cup Peanut Sauce (see recipe under Sauces
    and Dips)
Red bell pepper strips for garnish

Preheat oven to 275°F. Carefully remove salmon from can,
leaving the meat in about three 3-ounce pieces. Place pieces of
salmon on a baking sheet or other ovenproof bakeware. Place
in oven at 275°F just to get it hot. It is already cooked and does
not need further cooking.

In a large sauté pan, place ½ cup water. Bring to a boil over
high heat. Add spinach leaves. Using a pair of tongs, gently toss
the spinach leaves and move them to the hot spots in the pan
so that they gently wilt. Keep moving them around so they wilt
evenly. Remove from pan and divide among three warmed dinner plates, ½ cup spinach per plate. Place a piece of salmon on
top of the spinach, then pour ¼ cup of warmed peanut sauce
over the top. Garnish attractively with several thin slices of fresh
red bell pepper.

One serving, with Peanut Sauce—Calories: 230; Total fat: 10 g;
Total carbohydrates: 14 g; Protein: 25 g; Sodium: 660 mg

Salmon Burgers
Serves 4

2 eggs, beaten
1 cup panko (Japanese-style breadcrumbs) or seasoned breadcrumbs
4 teaspoons minced onion
8 ounces canned wild Alaska pink salmon, drained, bones and skin removed
4 hamburger buns

Combine eggs, breadcrumbs, and minced onion in a bowl. Gently fold in the salmon to combine well but don't overmix or the salmon will become mushy. Leave some nice chunks of muscle tissue. Form into four patties. Heat a small amount of oil in a heavy skillet. When the oil is hot, place the patties in it and fry over medium-low to medium heat for about 1 minute per side. They should get a nice, lightly browned color and heat through. Place on toasted or warmed hamburger buns and serve with desired accompaniments.

One serving—Calories: 300; Total fat: 8 g; Total carbohydrates: 35 g; Protein: 23 g; Sodium: 610 mg

Smoked Salmon Pizza with Caramelized Onions
Makes 1 12-inch round pizza (serves 6)

1 cup canned wild Alaska pink salmon, drained,
     bones and skin removed, in chunks
2 teaspoons liquid smoke flavor
3 plus 1 tablespoons butter
1 large red onion, halved and cut into thin slices
2 teaspoons granulated sugar
3 garlic cloves, mashed
2½ tablespoons flour
½ cup milk, warmed
⅛ teaspoon salt
1 prepared 12-inch round pizza dough

In a bowl, toss the salmon chunks with the smoke flavor. Let this sit and absorb the flavor while you cook the onions.

In a large fry pan, melt 3 tablespoons of the butter. Add the onion and sugar. Sauté over low heat until the onions soften and become a nice golden-brown color. Do not raise the heat very high, or the onions will brown too quickly and will not soften. This will take about 20 to 25 minutes.

Make a creamy garlic sauce by melting the remaining 1 tablespoon butter over low heat. Add the garlic and cook on low heat until it softens and becomes very aromatic. Add the flour and stir it in. Stir and cook for 2 minutes until the mixture looks like wet sand. Whisk in the warmed milk and salt.

Raise the heat to medium high. Stir constantly while the sauce thickens. When it comes to a boil, reduce the heat to low and simmer while stirring, about 3 minutes. Remove from heat, let cool slightly, then spread over the pizza dough. Sprinkle the smoked salmon over the sauce. Spread the onions evenly over the pizza.

Bake according to pizza-dough package directions.

One serving—Calories: 470; Total fat: 24 g; Total carbohydrates: 40 g; Protein: 27 g; Sodium: 970 mg

Salmon Rémoulade Salad
Serves 4

4 cups lettuce, washed and chopped
1 can (14.75 ounces) wild Alaska pink salmon,
    drained, bones and skin removed
2 fresh tomatoes, cut into wedges
½ cup Rémoulade Sauce (see recipe under Sauces
    and Dips)

Divide lettuce among four salad plates or bowls. Prepare equal portions of the salmon, then place flaked salmon on top of the lettuce. Arrange tomato wedges on salad and top with Rémoulade Sauce.

One serving, with Rémoulade Sauce—Calories: 220; Total fat: 14 g; Total carbohydrates: 6 g; Protein: 19 g; Sodium: 360 mg

BREADS AND DESSERTS

Artichoke Nut Bread
Makes 2 loaves (serves 20)

¾ cup milk
1 cup artichoke pulp
1 egg
¼ cup butter
2½ cups flour
¾ cup sugar
2 teaspoons baking powder
1 teaspoon baking soda
1 teaspoon cinnamon
1 teaspoon nutmeg
½ teaspoon salt
½ teaspoon fresh ginger, minced
1 cup walnuts, chopped

Preheat oven to 350°F. Combine the milk, artichoke pulp, and egg in a mixing bowl. Melt butter and add to milk mixture. In a separate mixing bowl, mix together the flour, sugar, baking powder, baking soda, cinnamon, nutmeg, salt, and ginger. Add the walnuts to the flour mixture and stir. Add the milk mixture and blend only until dry ingredients are moistened. Pour into two 4″ × 8″ loaf pans, greased lightly. Bake at 350°F for 55 minutes.

One slice (1¾ ounces)—Calories: 150; Total fat: 7 g; Total carbohydrates: 20 g; Protein: 3 g; Sodium: 210 mg

Pumpkin Bread
Makes 2 loaves (serves 32)

⅔ cup butter or trans-fat-free shortening
3 cups white sugar
4 eggs, beaten
2 cups canned or mashed pumpkin
3½ cups flour
⅔ cup walnuts, chopped
½ teaspoon baking powder
2 teaspoons baking soda
1 teaspoon cinnamon
½ teaspoon cloves
½ teaspoon salt
1 teaspoon vanilla

Preheat oven to 350°F. Cream butter with sugar; add eggs and mix. Add pumpkin, then the rest of the ingredients. Bake for 1 hour at 350°F in the oven.

One slice (2 ounces)—Calories: 160; Total fat: 6 g; Total carbohydrates: 25 g; Protein: 3 g; Sodium: 160 mg

Cranberry-Orange Bread
Makes 1 loaf (serves 12)

2 cups whole wheat flour
½ cup sugar
¼ cup nonfat dry milk powder
1 teaspoon baking powder
1 teaspoon baking soda
1 teaspoon salt
¼ cup butter, melted
2 eggs
1 cup unsweetened orange juice
¼ cup walnuts, chopped
1½ cups fresh cranberries, coarsely chopped
Vegetable cooking spray

Preheat the oven to 350°F. Combine flour, sugar, dry milk powder, baking powder, baking soda, and salt in a large bowl. Mix the butter, eggs, and orange juice in separate bowl. Add to the flour mixture, stirring just until moistened. Stir in the walnuts and cranberries.

Coat a 9½″ × 5½″ × 2¾″ loaf pan with the cooking spray, then spoon the batter gently into the pan. Bake at 350°F for 1 hour or until a toothpick inserted into the center comes out clean. Let cool in pan for at least 10 minutes, remove, and cool before slicing.

One serving—Calories: 180; Total fat: 7 g; Total carbohydrates: 26 g; Protein: 4 g; Sodium: 400 mg

Blueberry Nut Bread

Makes 1 loaf (serves 12)

1¼ cups unbleached flour
¼ cup whole wheat flour
½ teaspoon ground allspice
1 teaspoon baking powder
1 teaspoon baking soda
½ teaspoon salt
2 eggs
⅔ cup sugar
½ cup canola oil
1 teaspoon vanilla extract
½ cup canned crushed pineapple in natural juice,
    undrained
¼ cup chopped toasted walnuts
1½ cups fresh blueberries

Preheat oven to 350°F. In a bowl, combine unbleached and whole wheat flours, allspice, baking powder, baking soda, and salt.

In a mixing bowl, beat eggs and the sugar until fluffy, about 3 minutes. Beat in the oil and vanilla. Gently stir in the pineapple and its juice, nuts, and blueberries.

Pour into a 1½-quart loaf pan. Bake at 350°F in the oven for 1 hour. Cool before slicing.

One slice (2½ ounces)—Calories: 210; Total fat: 12 g; Total carbohydrates: 24 g; Protein: 3 g; Sodium: 260 mg

Blackberry Cobbler Rolls
Serves 10

1 cup plus 2 tablespoons sugar
1½ cups flour
¼ teaspoon salt
2¼ teaspoons baking powder
1 cup butter or margarine, divided into two ½-cup
    portions
⅓ cup milk, room temperature
2 cups fresh or frozen blackberries
½ teaspoon ground cinnamon

Preheat oven to 350°F. In a saucepan, heat 1 cup water and 1 cup of the sugar until the sugar melts; set aside. Put flour, salt, and baking powder into a mixing bowl; cut in half of the butter or margarine until the consistency is fine crumbs. Add milk and stir until dough leaves sides of bowl. Turn out onto a floured surface; knead three or four times. Roll out to an 11″ × 9″ rectangle ¼ inch thick. Spread blackberries over dough and sprinkle with cinnamon. Now roll up the dough lengthwise. Cut into 10 ¼-inch thick slices. In a 10-inch round or oval baking dish, melt the remaining ½ cup of the butter. Lay slices in baking dish over butter. Pour sugar syrup around slices; syrup will be absorbed. Bake at 350°F for 45 minutes. Sprinkle remaining sugar over the top and bake 15 minutes more. Serve warm or cold.

One serving—Calories: 300; Total fat: 19 g; Total carbohydrates: 34 g; Protein: 3 g; Sodium: 320 mg

Pineapple Upside-Down Cake
Serves 10

1 can (20 ounces) crushed pineapple with juice
3 tablespoons butter plus ⅓ cup butter
10 maraschino cherries
½ cup—or 10—walnut halves
⅔ packed cup brown sugar
½ cup white sugar
1 egg
1 teaspoon vanilla extract
1¼ cups sifted cake flour
1½ teaspoons baking powder
½ teaspoon salt
½ cup reserved pineapple juice

Preheat oven to 350°F. Drain pineapple and reserve ½ cup of the juice. Melt 3 tablespoons butter in a 9-inch round pan. Arrange cherries and walnut halves in the buttery pan, and then place the pineapple in the pan. Sprinkle with brown sugar.

In a mixing bowl, whisk together remaining butter and granulated sugar until light and fluffy. Add egg and vanilla, and beat well. Sift flour, baking powder, and salt. Add the flour mixture to the butter-sugar mixture alternately with reserved pineapple syrup, beating after each addition.

Spread batter in pan over pineapple. Bake at 350°F for 45 to 50 minutes. Let stand 5 minutes in the pan, then flip over onto plate. Serve warm.

One serving—Calories: 260; Total fat: 12 g; Total carbohydrates: 37 g; Protein: 3 g; Sodium: 140 mg

Blueberry Crisp
Serves 8

3 cups blueberries, fresh or frozen
¼ cup butter, softened
¾ cup plus ½ cup white sugar
1 cup flour
⅛ teaspoon salt
1½ teaspoons baking powder
½ cup milk
1 tablespoon cornstarch
¼ teaspoon ground nutmeg

Preheat the oven to 350°F. Fill a small saucepan with water and bring to boil while preparing recipe. Put the blueberries into an 8-inch square baking dish. In a bowl, whisk together the butter and ¾ cup white sugar until smooth. Stir the flour mixed with salt and baking powder into the butter mixture alternately with the milk. Spoon batter over blueberries. Mix together the remaining ½ cup sugar with the cornstarch and nutmeg. Sprinkle over the top of the blueberries. Pour 1 cup of the boiling water over the batter. Bake for 1 hour. Cool for at least 10 minutes to set. Serve with whipped topping or vanilla ice cream.

One serving—Calories: 230; Total fat: 6 g; Total carbohydrates: 47 g; Protein: 2 g; Sodium: 190 mg

Yogurt Smoothie with Fruit
Serves 2

6 ounces low-fat yogurt
1 cup 2 percent milk
1 cup frozen or fresh raspberries or other fruit
1 medium banana sliced or 1 cup other fruit

Place all ingredients in blender or food processor. Cover and blend on high for about 25 to 30 seconds or until smooth.

One serving—Calories: 190; Total fat: 3.5 g; Total carbohydrates: 35 g; Protein: 7 g; Sodium: 105 mg

Poached Peaches with Raspberry Sauce
Serves 8

8 large ripe peaches, all roughly the same size
¼ lemon, for juice
1 cup sugar
1 teaspoon vanilla
2 (10-ounce) packages of frozen raspberries
¾ cup jelly, preferably raspberry or cherry (or at
   least red)
1½ teaspoons potato starch
2 tablespoons framboise or other liqueur
1 quart low-fat vanilla ice cream

Put the peaches in a large pot of boiling water and leave for 20 seconds. Remove the peaches and drop into a bowl of cold water. Remove the peach skins and sprinkle lemon juice on the peaches.

In another pan, pour sugar, vanilla, and 1¼ cup water. Bring to a boil and place the peaches into pan to poach for about 6 to 8 minutes. Remove the peaches and cool them on a baking sheet. Once cooled, cut the peaches in half and remove the pit. Chill the peaches in the refrigerator.

Prepare the raspberry sauce by thawing the berries in a pan along with the jelly and bringing the mixture to a boil. Mix in 1 tablespoon cold water and the potato starch. Stir until the sauce is has cooked down. Add the framboise; stir for another minute. Strain the sauce and let cool.

When ready to serve, place peaches in eight dessert bowls.
Add a scoop of ice cream over each and cover with raspberry
sauce.

One serving—Calories: 360; Total fat: 2.5 g; Total carbohydrates: 82 g; Protein: 5 g; Sodium: 55 mg

10

Pioneering a Bold Future for Brain Health

*By turning inward with great curiosity and passion, we will not only
pioneer new understandings of the human brain, we will discover that
all of our answers are tucked deep inside our brain's folds and grooves.*

◉

Now that you know about the five critical domains of
brain health, it's time to take those practical suggestions
and tips and implement brain health in all areas of your life.
Remember that the five major components of the lifestyle are
socialization, physical activity, mental stimulation, spirituality,
and nutrition. In these areas, there are definitely proactive steps
you can take, backed by a growing body of research, to promote
brain health.

The fascinating fact about brain health is that we already
know what kinds of environments are likely to promote brain
health; we simply need to reorient our surrounding. Research

tells us that an environment that is enriched and provides novel and complex stimuli increases our potential for brain health by building brain reserve. This brain reserve is thought to help delay the onset of neurodegenerative diseases such as Alzheimer's, which helps to underscore the importance of a proactive and lifelong pursuit of brain health, as we all want to maintain our memories and life stories.

I have proposed implementation of a brain health lifestyle by first establishing brain health as a priority and desired cultural shift. Regardless of the setting or environment, such as school, workplace, and home, among others, the first step that must occur is both conceptual and informational. For those interested in your own brain health, it is critical that you become educated on the basics of your brain, how it operates, and how a proactive lifestyle can promote the health of your brain. This text articulates my brain health lifestyle as a tangible example of a proactive approach to brain health. There needs to be a belief that persons within the environment can engage in and benefit from activities and a general lifestyle that promote brain health.

For every entity that is interested in creating a brain-healthy culture, distinct individuals emerge who are quite eager to learn and lead the movement to brain health. I refer to these persons as "brain health ambassadors," and they become the core staff within the existing environment to foster and promote the change. Working closely with the brain health ambassadors, I can help to keep a strategic focus and direction for the team as the culture takes small but persistent steps toward brain health.

UNLOCKING THE POTENTIAL OF THE HUMAN BRAIN

It is tempting to try and discuss the brain in technical terms and to try and advance predictions of brain function that are highly theoretical. I generally believe the mystery of the human brain will be unlocked in basic and simplistic terms, with ideas that have a home more in the wisdom taught us by past generations than a university laboratory. We may be surprised to discover that the human brain can be best understood and shaped using simplistic approaches, and it is this simplistic beauty that makes the human brain truly remarkable. I think there is both complexity and parsimony in the human brain, which probably is the essence of its brilliance.

We have learned some basic truths about the human brain that can help us to dream about the brain of tomorrow. These truths include the following:

- The human brain is the most complicated and sophisticated system ever designed in the history of our universe.
- We do not understand much about the human brain, and we consistently underestimate its sheer capacity and power.
- The human brain has plasticity and can be shaped by environment across the life span.
- The human brain can develop new brain cells in the hippocampus and olfactory system. Interestingly, these two regions of the brain are close to one another, and we can all appreciate how memories that form in the hippocam-

pus can have a trigger from a sense of smell. The same
process of environmental stimulation that can lead to new
brain-cell development in the hippocampus likely affects
the olfactory neural networks.

- The brain can be stimulated for health at any age.
- The human brain responds favorably to enriched environments where the stimuli are novel and complex.
- A proactive and lifelong brain health lifestyle builds brain
  reserve important to delaying the onset of Alzheimer's and
  other dementias.

This understanding of the human brain is relatively new
and is significantly different from our traditional understanding
of our brain as a rigid, fixed, and essentially degrading system
from birth. We used to be entrenched in the idea of a "critical
period of brain development" that was fixed, and thus ended,
in childhood. Plasticity was not considered an established fact
for humans even though rodent brains evinced plasticity more
than fifty years ago. It is true that much has been learned about
the human brain in the past forty to fifty years, and the next
fifty years will provide us with an even greater understanding
of this critical part of our being.

Consider how the human species has evolved from a primitive being unable to communicate to an upright and mobile
animal capable of many languages. We have moved from
hunter-gatherer to astronaut. We used to rely on a telephone
with one line, and now we have the ability to send e-mail or text
messages across the planet in seconds. Air travel, space exploration, and discoveries under our oceans have provided us the
ability to live more efficiently and more productively. Most

significant is our ability to generate, acquire, and process more information today than at any other time in our history. All one has to do is look up an idea to realize how much information exists today. With all these advances, the rapid explosion of information, and the ongoing upgrades to technology, we must pause and reflect upon how such creation occurs. It is the human brain that permits such advancement, and it is the brain that responds to such advancements. It is a systematic dance that originates in the brain and returns to the brain in the form of a new technology or piece of information. It is from this interplay that the human brain grows, becomes more sophisticated, and enriches the human race.

What does all this mean for the future of our species, for the structure and function of our brain, and for improving the human condition? As a curious animal, the human being will continue to ask questions and to seek answers. We will improve our species by becoming more technologically advanced, more informed, and more capable of addressing those things that threaten our existence. Our brains will continue to grow, probably with increased cortical mass and an even larger frontal lobe. We will continue to develop new windows into the structure and function of the human brain that will provide us with a better understanding of how the brain works.

A New and Exciting World of Neural Energies

The future of the human brain is fascinating to consider. I believe the next decade will provide us insights into the power of the human brain that will yield a new frontier for new forms of communication, control of energy outside the body, and a new form of understanding as to how to manage and perhaps reverse illness inside the body. This appreciation of the brain as a brilliant and dynamic system of energy and the strategic exploration to tap and utilize this energy are what I call "neural energies." Our ability to utilize this power of our brain will advance our species in unprecedented ways.

The United States military is already conducting research on how soldiers on the front line can communicate with other soldiers mentally, without opening the mouth. Case studies have described persons paralyzed with no ability to speak or move who maintain communication skills in the form of electrical energy. That is, these individuals have been taught to use their thoughts to create electrical energy that is transmitted across electrodes placed on the skull and into a computer in which a cursor moves over particular letters to form a sentence. I recently read a report on the relationship between deep meditation and slowing of HIV. Plenty of studies exist on the relationship between prayer and positive outcomes in surgery, positive attitude and successful outcomes with a particular illness, and even a relationship between humor and positive health. We do not understand how placebo works, but we do know that most studies will yield a 25 percent positive outcome for patients placed in a placebo group. Placebo might actually be a misunderstood form of treatment.

Such findings exist today, and though we cannot explain them very well, they seem to underscore the power of the mind to manage or manipulate the body. Sports psychology is a growing field of expertise, as the world's best athletes recognize the value in visualization, relaxation, focus, and mentally creating success for physical performance. Indeed, an argument can be made that the difference between the greatest athletes and other professional athletes is their mental discipline and ability to focus at the highest level. Their brains do not get distracted, and anxiety does not alter their physical performance. Otherwise, there is very little difference between professional athletes when comparing physical attributes or performance mechanics.

The future pioneers of the human brain will explore neural energies and how the electrical forces from such energies can control matter within and outside the body. This has enormous potential value for health care, as it can unleash completely noninvasive methods to treat disorders throughout the body. It also has enormous value for communication and will potentially enable immediate interaction between any two or more people on the planet. Neural energies could transform the body within and enable interpersonal interaction in almost real time. Neural energies may shape our species for many years.

Turning Inward for Answers

Perhaps as new methodologies emerge to explore and unleash the powers of the human brain, we will discover new talents and remedies to our most pressing needs. We may learn how our neural energy can routinely regulate our bodies to homeostasis with balanced levels of sugar and blood pressure. Cures for cancer, Alzheimer's, mental illness, and substance abuse may indeed be found in a piece of bark deep in the Amazon Jungle. The cure may just as reasonably be found in the deep gyri of one brain of the billions of brains on our planet. Remember, it only takes one brain for something to be considered real or possible. I have a fundamental belief that the human brain contains the answers to our greatest difficulties, our most challenging questions. The brain is simply too brilliant to not provide us the roadmaps to different solutions, to make life on Earth a better experience, and to wipe disabling diseases from our existence. The brain contains the mathematical wizardry necessary to create the twenty-second-century world and to appreciate deeply complex things such as time and aging itself. The brain seeks pleasure, and its most elegant processing occurs when it is stimulated using multiple sensory pathways simultaneously. The brain also contains answers so that all people of different backgrounds with different sets of beliefs can appreciate more fully we are one species with more similarity than difference.

Our future holds significant promise for an entirely new understanding of the human brain. As we develop more sophisticated means of exploring the human brain, we will begin to close the gap between what we now believe about the human brain and what is real. We continue to underestimate the power of the brain because we do not understand it well enough. There is a basic human tendency to be cautious and dubious, but I believe we should be aggressive and bold with regard to the potential of the human brain. The future will provide us with more insight and a deeper appreciation for how brilliant the brain is. We will also learn how to use our brains in new and highly efficient ways and to adapt to life circumstances in ways that increase our health and longevity. Perhaps we will also discover within our brain the deep sense of spirituality that has existed in humans since the beginning of time. We may even find that the complexities, questions, and answers on the origin of our universe are the same for the brain. Can something so brilliant be random?

Until such exploration yields some of these insights, we need to begin the process of learning about our own brain. From a basic understanding of your brain, you can understand why a proactive lifestyle is critical. Personalizing the message of this book will enable you to engage in a brain health lifestyle across your entire life span, which is desirable because the goal of maintaining access to your life story is so meaningful. It is important to try and reflect on the many brilliant things you do every day, the experiences of life, and the social interactions your brain permits you to experience. We are truly blessed to have such a complicated and miraculous system within our skull. We are also so fortunate to have the ability to shape our brains, which means we have some control over the integrity and indeed the health of our brain. This is truly a wonderful opportunity for each of us to engage in the proactive path toward brain health. You have been encoding experiences most of your life, and your brain has placed them systematically into a long-term storage for your use. I refer to this as your autobiography, *your life story*, the most precious gift you have. It is critical that you maintain access to your life story so you can share it with your next great generation, the little ones in your life. Get started on your journey toward brain health today. You have much to share!

A FINAL WORD

Brain health is a critically important and interesting frontier that has captured the focus of the nation and the world. It is now up to those of us on the front lines of schools, libraries, homes, and corporations to introduce and implement brain health. Everyone who works to learn about their brain and to make lifestyle changes to promote their own brain health will benefit. While change is typically not easy, such lifestyle alterations can be fun and personally relevant. It is time for all of us to begin a proactive approach to protecting our life stories so that we can share them with our next great generation of little ones!

Good luck with your own journey to better brain health!

Resources

◉

Paul D. Nussbaum, Ph.D.
paulnussbaum.com
drnuss@zoominternet.net
412-471-1195

Dr. Nussbaum's website offers a tremendous amount of friendly information on the human brain and brain health promotion. He also provides a series of links to different companies that he works with and programs and products on brain health. You can also order Dr. Nussbaum's books on his brain health lifestyle and DVDs.

Kathy Rusk, Registered Dietitian
Nutrition Dynamics Northwest
nutritiondynamicsnw.com
kathy@nutritiondynamicsnw.com
425-269-6979

Websites

Moxxor Nutritional Supplements
mymoxxor.com/drpaul

The Moxxor website offers great information on nutritional supplements that can help boost brain health.

Fit Brains
fitbrains.com

Fit Brains provides fun and friendly brain-fitness games that give you a daily brain workout. Fit Brains also provides useful tools to help you get started on a brain health lifestyle. Dr. Nussbaum serves as the chief scientific officer to Fitbrains, Inc.

Emeritus Senior Living
emeritus.com

Emeritus is one of the largest assisted-living companies in the United States, and it has incorporated Dr. Nussbaum's brain health lifestyle into its culture. Dr. Nussbaum works closely with Emeritus to provide superior programs for residents in independent-living, assisted-living, and memory-care situations.

International Center for Leadership in Education
leadered.com

The International Center for Leadership in Education is a leading authority on education and necessary reforms for improving the education system in America. Dr. Nussbaum serves ICLE as a senior advisor for brain health and education, and he provides keynote presentations to school districts across the country.

Alzheimer's Prevention
alzprevention.org

The Alzheimer's Foundation of America provides information and programs on research-based methods to delay the onset of Alzheimer's and related dementias. Dr. Nussbaum serves as the chair of the Prevention Advisory Board for AFA.

Connected Living
mywayvillage.com

MyWay Village has a unique program called Connected Living that provides seniors with computer-based methods to tell their life stories and to remain integrated with family and friends. Dr. Nussbaum serves as the chief brain health officer and provides leadership to MyWay Village on aspects of brain health and the importance of socialization as one component to a brain health lifestyle.

American Society on Aging

asaging.org

The American Society on Aging is a leading organization for education and training in nearly all aspects of aging. Dr. Nussbaum has worked with the ASA to provide keynote presentations on brain health for many years.

Marbles

marblesthebrainstore.com

This new and unique retail chain provides the consumer with some of the latest products and information dealing with brain health.

BOOKS ON BRAIN HEALTH

Brizendine, L. *The Female Brain*. New York: Morgan Road Books, 2006.

Carper, J. *Your Miracle Brain*. New York: Quill, 2001.

Diamond, M.C., & Hopson, J. *Magic Trees of the Mind*. New York: Plume, 1999.

Kotulak, R. *Inside the Brain: Revolutionary Discoveries of How the Mind Works*. Kansas City, MO: Anreas and McMeely, 1997.

Nussbaum, J.F., Federowicz, M., & Nussbaum, P.D. *Brain Health and Optimal Engagement in Older Adulthood*. Girona, Spain: Editorial Aresta, 2009.

Nussbaum, P.D. *Brain Health and Wellness.* Tarentum, PA: Word Association Publishing, 2003.

———. *Your Brain Health Lifestyle.* Tarentum, PA: Word Association Publishing, 2007.

———. *Your Brain Health Lifestyle: Application to the School, Library, Corporate and Business Setting, and Home.* 2nd ed. Tarentum, PA: Word Association Publishing, 2009.

Snowdon, D.A. *Aging with Grace.* New York: Bantam Books, 2001.

Snyder, P.J., Nussbaum, P.D., & Robins, D.L. *Clinical Neuropsychology: A Pocket Handbook for Assessment.* 2nd ed. Washington, DC: American Psychological Association, 2006.

RESEARCH PAPERS ON BRAIN HEALTH

Colcombe, S.J., et al. (2006). Aerobic exercise training increases brain volume in aging humans. *The Journal of Gerontology: Medical Sciences* 61:1166–70.

Diamond, M.C., Krech, D., & Rosenzweig, M.R. (1964). The effects of an enriched environment on the histology of the rat cerebral cortex. *Journal of Comparative Neurology* 123: 111–20.

Eriksson, P.S., Perfilieva, E., Bjork-Eriksson, T., Alborn, A.M., Nordborg, C., Peterson, D.A., & Gage, F.H. (1998). Neurogenesis in the adult human hippocampus. *Nature Medicine* 4:1313–17.

Mortimer, J.A. (1997). Brain reserve and the clinical expression of Alzheimer's disease. *Geriatrics* 52:S50–S53.

Snowdon, D.A., Kemper, S.J., Mortimer, J.A., Greiner, L.H., Wekstein, D.R., & Markesbery, W.R. (1996). Linguistic ability in early life and cognitive function and Alzheimer's disease in late life: Findings from the nun study. *Journal of the American Medical Association* 275:528–32.

Willis, S.L., et al. (2006). Long-term effects of cognitive training on everyday functional outcomes in older adults. *JAMA* 296:2805–14.

ADDITIONAL REFERENCES
ON NUTRITION

DHA, A Good Fat. American Dietetic Association Fact Sheet. Chicago, 2008.

The Human Brain—Fats, Micronutrients, and Proteins. Published on the Franklin Institute Resources for Science Learning website (http://www.fi.edu/learn/brain/fats.html, http://www.fi.edu/learn/brain/micro.html, http://www.fi.edu/learn/brain/proteins.html), 2004.

Omega-3 Fatty Acids, Fish Oil, Alpha-Linolenic Acid. Natural Standard Patient Monograph, published on the Mayo

Clinic website by the Mayo Foundation for Medical Education and Research, June 20, 2008.

Omega-6 Fatty Acids and Risk for Cardiovascular Disease. The American Heart Association, Harris, W., et al. *Circulation* 2009, 119:902–907.

Mahon, K., & Stump, S.E. *Krause's Food, Nutrition and Diet Therapy.* W.B. Saunders, 2003.

Schmidt, Michael A. *Brain-Building Nutrition: How Dietary Fats and Oils Affect Mental, Physical, and Emotional Intelligence.* 3rd ed. Frog Books, Ltd., 2007.

Tribole, E. *The Ultimate Omega-3 Diet.* McGraw-Hill, 2007.

INDEX

⊙